The Theatre Student

PHYSICAL MOVEMENT

FOR THE THEATRE

 THE THEATRE STUDENT SERIES

The Theatre Student

PHYSICAL MOVEMENT FOR THE THEATRE

Peter Kline
and
Nancy Meadors

Illustrations by Harold Isen

PUBLISHED BY

RICHARDS ROSEN PRESS, INC.

NEW YORK, N.Y. 10010

Standard Book Number: 8239–0235–8
Library of Congress Catalog Card Number: 74–146703
Dewey Decimal Classification: 791

Published in 1971 by Richards Rosen Press, Inc.
29 East 21st Street, New York City, N.Y. 10010

Copyright 1971 by Peter Kline and Nancy Meadors

Revised Edition

Manufactured in the United States of America

DEDICATION

For Amiel W. Francke
and
Beatrice E. Richardson
without whose detailed inspiration this book could not
have been written

ABOUT THE AUTHORS

PETER KLINE and NANCY MEADORS developed this book on the basis of a course they taught together at Sandy Spring Friends School, where Mr. Kline was head of the English and drama departments, and Miss Meadors taught English and was founder of the dance department.

Mr. Kline has also been head of the English department at the Maret School and now teaches English at Sidwell Friends. He has taught acting to students of all ages, and has been active in community and educational theatre work for twenty years. He is the author of three other books in this series: *Scenes to Perform, Playwriting,* and *Gilbert and Sullivan Production.* He received his B.A. from Amherst College and his M.A. from Catholic University.

Miss Meadors has had extensive experience in dance education and has worked on several theatrical productions as a coach of physical movement. She believes that dance and drama have educational value in the development of personality, and has consequently made use of them in her work as an English teacher. She received her B.A. from Scripps College, and is now a teacher at the Madeira School.

HAROLD ISEN (illustrator) is a graphic artist and sculptor. After receiving his M.F.A. from Pratt Institute in New York, Mr. Isen taught at the Corcoran School of Art in Washington, D.C., and is at present assistant professor of art at the University of Maryland. Mr. Isen has done numerous illustrations and designs for books, magazines, newspapers, National Educational Television, and theatre. His work is represented in the permanent collections of the Library of Congress, the National Library of Medicine, the Corcoran Gallery of Art, the National Collection of Fine Arts, and the San Francisco Museum of Art. Mr. Isen has a beautiful and talented wife named Anita and a gentle German Shepherd named Bunthorne.

PREFACE

Because of its relationship to the words of a printed play, the art of acting has too often emphasized the vocal skills of the performer out of proportion to the communicative qualities of his body. That emphasis has been reinforced in America by the frequent association of drama departments in universities with speech departments. Corresponding association with dance departments has been infrequent, so that the relationship between drama and dance is seldom pursued very far. Furthermore, the great emphasis on the training of emotions in some schools of acting often draws attention even further away from the communicative function and proper discipline of the body.

We offer this book in the hope that it will solve a problem faced by many instructors of drama whose training has been primarily in oral communication. The book is designed to provide exercises that will increase the flexibility and communicative skills of the body and thus help the actor to support the vocal and emotional aspects of his art with controlled movement. The book is intended to be used by the student on his own or in conjunction with a class. It may be used by the beginner or the aspiring professional, as it includes both basic exercises designed to improve coordination and others designed for specific dramatic situations and problems of characterization.

Merely by reading through the book a student can gain enough insight into the communicative potential of his body to make significant improvement in his work as an actor. If he goes further and develops a program for himself based on the exercises we have provided, he should be able to broaden his scope enough so that he can perform roles previously beyond his grasp. We hope that classes in colleges and high schools, as well as students and professionals who are working on their own, will derive inspiration from this book.

The authors would like to thank the colleagues and students by whose thinking we have been consciously or unconsciously influenced. We are particularly grateful to Lynn Sherwood for her helpful comments on the manuscript. We are also indebted to the following students at Sandy Spring Friends School, who posed for pictures: Ronlyn Arnatt, Sabina Barach, Carole Brooks, Ellen Campbell, Ted Davis, Adrienne Gant, Michael Garin, Elizabeth Iribe, Margery Lanagan, Marian Lobred, Marc Long, Sarah McClelland, Craig North, Maria Sanchez, Lisa Sutton, Priscilla Taylor, Tyrone Thomas, and Lisa Yntema.

Peter Kline
Nancy Meadors

CONTENTS

INTRODUCTION

Acting is a process of taking words that someone has written down and translating them into human beings. If you are an actor, you are an instrument for conveying the words of a playwright to an audience. It is the purpose of this book to help you explore the many ways in which words can be brought to life through actions that reinforce and amplify their meaning. Using the body to mirror the action of the mind requires skill both in exploring the motivations of a character and in expressing those motivations in actions that are harmonious with the words being spoken. As you work with some of the exercises we have designed for you, you should become more critical of the way in which you express verbal meanings nonverbally.

Dr. Albert Mehrabian, in an article entitled "Communication Without Words," [1] has pointed out that most of the messages we convey to one another are nonverbally expressed. In any communication process between human beings, 7 percent of the meaning is transmitted by the words used, 38 percent by the tone of voice in which they are spoken, and 55 percent by the nonverbal behavior of the speaker. He writes, "A great many forms of nonverbal behavior can communicate feeling: touching, facial expression, tone of voice, spatial distance from the addressee, relaxation of posture, rate of speech, number of errors in speech." We may conclude from such studies that in a play the actor has the opportunity to convey far more of the message than the playwright does.

Few actors take the fullest advantage of their opportunity to communicate. Since more than half of the message is conveyed by the body, it is extremely important that the actor make his body as subtle and expressive in movement as possible. The actor who can delve deeply into the thought processes and emotions of the character and convey them not only in the way he speaks his lines, but also in the way he moves while speaking them, is the actor who is exploring the possibilities of his art most fully. It is the purpose of this book to help the actor mold his body into a tool of expression. We have provided a series of exercises designed to make the body more flexible so that in rehearsal it will serve the actor's purposes as well as possible. If you apply the exercises in this book, you will learn how to make your body a reflection of your thoughts. In the process you should enrich your creative approach to acting, as in the interplay between mind and body each enhances the expressiveness of the other.

"How can we know the dancer from the dance?" asks the poet William Butler Yeats. In fact, we cannot. We are so much the cumulative effect of what we do that it is impossible to separate our selves from our actions. The character in a play *is* what he *does,* and what he does, therefore, must be fully realized by the actor in its subtlest aspects. Think for a moment about how

---

[1] Mehrabian, Albert. "Communication Without Words," *Psychology Today,* September, 1968, p. 53.

your own body speaks. As surely as your voice conveys a message, so does a hand, a finger, or a tilt of the head. Many times a day you use movement to enhance or replace speech. The natural movement of your body makes clear a positive or negative answer before a "yes" or "no" can be uttered. Many times a day you say, "I don't know" without using the words. Before you can possibly get the words out, your instructor knows that you do not know the answer to his question. He also knows when an answer is not forthcoming because you are afraid. He knows, not because he has been told in words, but because the movement of your body states quite plainly how you feel. By squirming, biting your lips, or hunching your shoulders, you have told him more than you could say in words.

More subtle is the movement you use to reveal the kind of person you are. A muscle can contradict your words and shout a truth you want to conceal. Without knowing it, you may be saying, "I'm shy," "I'm ill at ease," "I'm nervous," or "I'm guilty." You also use your body to say many things about the relationship between you and the person you are talking to. If your posture is stiff or excessively relaxed, you may be indicating dislike. If your posture seems natural, you are probably feeling friendly toward the other person. If you stand directly facing him and look into his eyes, you may be indicating your desire for a close relationship with him. Awkwardness in the relationship might be indicated by angling your body away from him and looking at the floor.

Perhaps you can see that in the staging of a play it is important whether a particular line is spoken as the actor stands stiffly gazing at another actor from across the room or as he slumps in a chair next to him, looking at the floor. An actor may use his body to belie what he says with his voice. Intentional use of such technique adds to the depth and irony of characterization. Unintentional use of it is often the mark of rank amateurism. We have all seen performances in which a boy says to a girl, "I love you," and the audience breaks into hysterics. Probably he has spoken in a tone that conveys something like, "I think you're the ickiest girl I ever met, and I *hate* having to say this line." Meanwhile his body is saying, "I feel creepy as hell up here on the stage, but you ought to see me run for a touchdown." The audience is getting three separate messages, each of which to some extent contradicts the others. The incongruity between them is wildly funny. "I love you" is only 7 percent of what is being said, and the poor playwright is lost in the shuffle.

Just as one's body reflects attitudes, so it reflects thoughts. It is impossible to think any kind of thought without its being reflected in some way in the body. Even our dreams are always accompanied by rapid eye movements. Because we are instinctively aware that our bodies give away what our minds are thinking, we learn as we grow older to counteract the tendency by causing the body to restrict or change its behavior as we think. Even those counteractions are an important means of revealing what we are thinking. In other words, the body may say as much by what it does not do as by what it does. Thus the mind-body relationship may be extraordinarily subtle and complex, but it is always operating.

As an actor you should explore the many ways a particular set of words may cause a character to behave, both vocally and physically. You must gradually make of your body an instrument on which can be played any behavior that is appropriate. In order to do so, your body must explore a wide range of physical patterns. You need to build up reserves on which you can draw as you need them for a particular character.

When we speak of reserves, we mean abilities that are drawn upon but never fully exploited. To understand the concept, suppose that you have to lift two things. One of them is a safety pin. You can lift it very easily, and so there are many options available to you as to the manner in which you do so. You might lift it gracefully or quickly or slowly or angrily: any way you choose. But now you are asked to lift a large object weighing seventy-five pounds. You can do that also, but you must put a lot more of yourself into it, and consequently you will not have many choices as to how you perform the task. The more we have any particular skill in reserve, the more we are in the position of the person lifting a safety pin. In other words, the more options we have as to how we will exercise that skill. Consequently, it will always be true that the greatest actors do far more in their practice sessions than they ever do in performance. They build the reserves that are needed to expand their options in whatever they do, and to give them grace and flexibility in doing it. They always have so many choices as to how they will do a thing that the most appropriate way of doing it can be selected.

As you work through the exercises in this book, you will build up reserves of physical skill upon which you can later draw in performing a particular role. The greater your reserves, the greater your performance may become.

We shall be concerned with four levels of developing physical performance. As an actor performing a role you make simultaneous use of all four. Let us consider them in the reverse of the order in which they are developed.

The most obvious level is that of the immediate action. This is performed as the character would perform it. If you are opening a letter, you will do so differently depending on whether you are an old man or a dashing young lover. You must discover the best way of performing each immediate action in terms of the character you are playing.

The next level is that of character in general. How does it feel to be the character you are playing? How does he walk? How does he sit down? How does he move his hands? These things must be decided in general, and must be consistent throughout the performance of the role. They are habits of the character that are not limited to any particular action.

The third level is the general imaginative character of your behavior as an actor, or your personal style. No matter how skillful an actor is, it is always possible to distinguish his particular mannerisms from those of any other actor. Some actors create electricity just by walking onstage. Others cannot be exciting to watch no matter what they do. As an actor you will develop a style of physical behavior that will form the outside limits of what you can do in any role you play. You should want your style to be as imaginative and rich as you can make it.

The fourth level is that of your general physical coordination. Your body has a number of information-receiving and -transmitting systems. By "system" we mean a group of parts of something that are so interconnected that what affects one part affects some or all of the other parts as well. The systems include your visual system, your speech-auditory system, and your system of balance. The way in which these systems operate within themselves and interact with one another determines the quality of your general physical behavior. To make this clearer, let us give an example.

When you first learned to walk you found it relatively difficult to stand up. Now you stand with no trouble at all. But if you were placed on a tightrope, you would suddenly find things much more difficult. Your system of balance has been trained to deal with the situations in which you usually find yourself. It could easily be much better trained than it is. You will improve your ability to move about on the stage in the attitudes of many varied characters if you improve your system of balance.

Once rehearsals for a play have begun, an actor works almost entirely on the first two levels of physical performance and must ignore the other two. It is in his overall training as an actor that he must develop the more basic skills. In this book we shall try to show you how to develop your skills equally on all four levels so that you can not only approach an individual role intelligently, but also improve your overall quality as an actor who aspires to more demanding roles. Although many of the exercises with which we shall be concerned may seem at first as mechanical as physical-fitness exercises, they will begin to become effective only as you learn to see them as keys to the understanding of human character. Although we shall speak primarily in terms of the body, we shall always be concerned with the body as a reflection of the mind, as the only true means by which the mind of one individual can be revealed to another.

PART I—YOU AND YOUR COORDINATION

Chapter I

HOW WE LEARN ABOUT MOVEMENT

In order to learn we must have information, and information comes to us through our senses. In this chapter we shall consider the sensory systems through which we gain information, and the kind of information that is brought to us through each. We shall also see how these systems work together to help us learn.

As a child you probably learned that you have five senses: seeing, hearing, tasting, touching, and smelling. For our purposes there are two additional important ones, which we shall call kinesthesia and balance. Since most people do not develop their senses of taste, touch, and smell very much, these are not ordinarily important sources of information; and we shall not consider them nearly as much as we shall consider the other four. Let us see now how the four basic sensory systems are developed.

Long before you were born you began to learn. What you learned was the most basic and intense learning you will ever do. You began to learn your own body. It was only a beginning of a process that even now you have far from completed. Somewhere in the darkness you began to sense that you had arms and legs and a trunk and a head—perhaps that much, and certainly no more than that. The greatness of that discovery is hard for you to imagine, now that you take these things for granted; but it was a truly great discovery, for it was a discovery that in the midst of *nothing* there was *something*. You did not distinguish at first between what was you and what was not-you. You had no sense of separate being.

At some time early in your life you began to separate the "not-me" from the "me." You began to be aware that you could move and feel, and what you could feel moving was "me," and what you could not feel moving was "not-me." The feeling you were beginning to discover is called *kinesthesia* or kinesthetic sense. It is the sense of one's own body in space. It is the most important sense we have, and the one upon which any performing artist is most heavily reliant. As your kinesthetic sense develops, you become more conscious of where you are in space, and you also become more conscious of the way in which various parts of your body interrelate. When you began to decide that what could be felt kinesthetically was "me," you laid the foundation for the sense of self that you have today. Now as you think the word "me" you may have some ideas about what that is, but you also have a total feeling that is in your body, and that cannot be expressed in words. That feeling is the summation of your kinesthetic experiences.

If you have ever watched a new-born infant while he is awake, you know that the arms and legs move in a somewhat circular but random motion. If you watch the eyes of a very young child, you will see that they are continually discovering and losing things, but that from time to time the child will become fascinated with some part of his own body. He does not yet know that there is any relation between what he sees and what he feels kinesthetically. In other words, what is visually his arm is not the same as what feels like his arm. He does not yet know that he is looking at himself. As time goes on, he will discover that the visual impressions and the kinesthetic impressions go together, and he will begin to connect them to form a sense of one thing, which he will then begin to sense can be named. An arm. A leg. A toe. Later, looking into a mirror, he will discover that, like other people, he has a nose, a mouth, and eyes. He is putting things together in his mind like building blocks, and those building blocks are beginning to form his impression of his own body.

Sometime, too, he will begin to sense that the noises that come out of him can be produced at will. He will make a connection between the sounds that he hears and the sounds that he can make. He will become able to imitate sounds made by others. He will become so fascinated with this that with extraordinary rapidity he will begin to learn a language. But he will learn more than just a language. He will learn that the sounds he makes express emotions, and those emotions affect the feelings of others. He will learn that with those sounds he can manipulate other people by asking them to bring him things or by expressing affection as a means of attracting them toward himself, or hostility as a means of driving them away. He will gain a tremendous feeling of power from that realization.

As he is using his voice to do things, so also he will use his body to do them. He will begin rocking back and forth, sensing that his whole body is one thing. Soon he will begin to crawl. That is easy enough, and seems to come naturally. But the great adventure is standing up and beginning to walk. That is not nearly so natural, for to do that is to defy gravity. His first few steps will be a perilous adventure. Often, during those

first few months, he will inexplicably topple over. Sometimes that will make him feel so defeated by the world that he will have to be put to bed. Other times he will be ready to try again, undaunted.

In all of the things he is doing, the infant child is learning to get along in, and to a certain extent to control, his world. What was chaos becomes order. As he brings order into his own body, the world around him also begins to seem orderly. The sense of order grows at the same rate on the inside as on the outside of a person. Sometimes it may stop growing or be reversed. If he is sick or threatened or moved into a new environment, the baby may lose the feeling of order he has so recently gained, and that may be hard for him to bear. But he will bear it and soon begin building his sense of order again.

As we think about how a young child learns his body and the world in which he lives and moves, we must realize how much that learning is his own. He does not grow into the world by instinct. Each step taken in the development of his awareness represents the solution to a problem just as surely as if he were solving problems in addition or subtraction. He will not learn if he does not try. But something in him makes him want to try again and again and again. His desire to learn is overwhelming and almost irresistible. By the time children have reached their teens it is often difficult to get them to learn anything. But it is practically impossible to stop a new baby from learning. He fills his empty mind as hungrily as if it were an empty stomach. But each child fills his mind in his own way. No one else has ever learned his body in quite the same way. No one else has quite the same impressions of how the world is organized. It is in his body sense that he first begins to be an individual.

Think about the implications of that for you, the actor, who must create characters quite unlike yourself. You are going to portray people who did not learn about their bodies and about the world in the same way that you did. It feels different to be someone else. In order to portray someone else on the stage, you will have to discover that difference in feeling.

Let us consider a couple of dramatic examples in order to make clearer what we mean. Bear in mind that for the sake of clarity we are vastly oversimplifying what really happens, as experiences may contradict or reinforce one another as one grows older, and no experience can have a decisive influence entirely on its own. Nevertheless, consider the following case. Imagine yourself a little child. You are crawling along the floor. You see a large, soft black thing. You crawl toward it and touch it. Suddenly it leaps up and you hear a noise and feel sharp pain in your body. How do you react? You are afraid, of course, but what does fear mean *inside* your body? Perhaps you draw back suddenly. Your stomach goes tight. You feel torn in many directions as you try to escape something that seems to be coming at you from no particular place. Next time you see that soft black thing you will anticipate what may happen to you, and your body will react the same way. As you grow older, if the experience is not contradicted by other more pleasant ones, you may always have that reaction inside you—a tightness and a feeling that you are falling apart. You will experience fear in those special physical terms.

Two people stand next to each other. A black cocker spaniel comes up to them, wagging its tail. One feels warmth and affection and wants to lean forward to pet it. The other feels what we have just described. It would be difficult for him to express any kind of affection. Do they see the same thing? The cocker spaniel is the same, but each of the two experiences it differently because each of them has built for himself his own particular world in which to live. Not only does it not look the same, it doesn't even *feel* the same. If you were watching those two people you would be able to see

the difference in their feelings. If you watched carefully, you might know how it feels to each of them to look at a cocker spaniel.

Imagine another example: You are a baby and you have discovered the joy of standing up holding onto something. One day you feel a desire to explore. Perhaps you can let go of what you are holding onto and take a step, just as you have seen older people do. You do so. You take one step and it is very exciting. You take another. Suddenly a hard piece of wood flies up and hits you in the face. Then another and another, and you are flying through the air and striking board after board. Finally you come to rest. You are hurting all over. You are screaming as loud as you can. No one comes. For what seems the longest time you have ever known you lie at the bottom of the stairs screaming.

If we observe two people standing at the top of a staircase looking down and one of them had in his childhood the experience we have just described, we may be able to see a difference in the way looking down that staircase *feels* to each of them.

As you look at the world, you feel various emotions, depending on what you are looking at. Your reaction in each case is reflected in a different posture. An overall feeling, however, determines the posture that characterizes you. Everyone has a distinctive posture; it is one of the first things you notice about anyone. Therefore, it is one of the most important things you can use to portray character. You need the posture that naturally grows out of how it feels for that character to look at the world he has built for himself.

We have talked a little about building a world for yourself, and we have mentioned that it is put together like building blocks. But that analogy does not take us far enough. One of the most important concepts in this book, and one of the most important concepts you have to deal with in becoming an actor, is the concept of *whole-*

ness. We have often heard that the whole is greater than the sum of its parts. Let us consider what that means and how one goes about building for oneself a whole world that is greater than the sum of its parts.

Imagine yourself walking down the street. You know you are walking, but do you think about it? Of course not. You are thinking about where you are going, or about what you will do today, or you are simply daydreaming. You stumble. Do you think about walking now? Of course you do. You have broken the rhythm of walking. You have broken something that is one thing into its parts. You pay attention long enough to put it together again.

When you first learned to walk, you put walking together. You do not remember it now, but when you took your first steps you had to take each one by itself. You can get that same sensation back again by walking on stilts, if you have never tried it before. It would take you a while before you could take a step at all. For a time each step would be something you would need to think about. After you pursued the exercise awhile you would find that you could walk on stilts just about as comfortably as you can walk without them, and you would stop thinking about the process and think about other things instead.

Gradually, during the learning process, the parts merge together and become the whole. It is interesting how that happens. It occurs in flashes of insight, but they do not occur all at the same time. You are concentrating on doing something, understanding each aspect of what you are doing. You have not yet put everything together, however, so that you feel comfortable with what you are doing. Then you get a sudden feeling that you know how the whole thing fits together. That doesn't last long, and pretty soon you are again struggling with the parts of the process while trying to remember the feeling that came and went so quickly. A little later there comes another flash of insight. The flashes recur more frequently until you have mastered the operation and cannot remember what it was like not to know how to do it.

As we grow up we learn many operations that reflect our personality. The way we walk, the way we sit down, how and when we smile, how we shake hands—all are done without thinking, and each of them is in a style unique to the person doing them. Furthermore, many of the simple actions we learn become the basis for more complex actions. Walking provides the foundation for running, skipping, hopping, jumping, and riding a bicycle. Manipulation of objects in the hand later leads to writing, playing musical instruments, playing baseball, and painting pictures. The way we do the simple things affects how we will do those that are more complex. And as we learn to do more complex things, we continue to structure our world so that as we grow older it continues to look and feel changed. We can imagine, perhaps, how the world looks to the nearsighted Mr. Magoo. But how does it look to a great painter or a great athlete? What does the physicist see when he looks at a waterfall that is different from what a poet sees? How does it *feel* to see various things? How do you look to others if you are a physicist rather than a poet looking at a waterfall? Such questions are important to an actor in the preparation of a particular characterization. The feelings that distinguish people from one another are subtle, and their interpretation is difficult, but great actors capture them and project them for all to see.

Let us talk now more specifically about some of the systems that our body uses to organize the world and help us to feel it as we do. If we understand how those systems operate, we shall be in a better position to train our bodies to communicate a variety of moods and emotions.

We have so far been talking mostly about the kinesthetic system. All of the muscles in your body can tell you how they feel and where they are in space, but they will do so only to the extent that you train them to communicate with you. You can easily do many things with your fingers. How many can you do with your toes? Can you wiggle each of your toes independently in turn? If not, it is not because your toes are inadequately equipped with nerves, but because you have not trained them to be sensitive to your commands. The same is true of all the other muscles in your body. They will do whatever you train them to do. You can sensitize them through exercise.

Suppose you are playing a man who has gout. Gout is a disease of the joints that causes painful inflammation. Sometimes it causes swelling in the toes, making it painful to walk on them. A person with gout in his toes will reorganize his whole walk around avoiding the pain of putting pressure on them. Gradually he will learn to do so without thinking about it and will develop a characteristic walk. If your feet are sensitive enough to your commands, you can imitate such a walk easily and immediately capture the attitude of a man with gout well enough so that an audience can see how it feels to walk in that manner.

The number of ways in which the various muscles in your body can work together is, for practical purposes, infinite. You should explore some of the possibilities. If you have practiced scales on the piano you know how easy it is to tell when the fingers of both hands are not working together. Can you get one finger and one toe to work together with the same exactness? When you walk do you swing your arms in rhythm with the way your legs move? Can you make a shoulder and a hip reflect that rhythm without moving the rest of the body? Can you make connections in your body between oddly assorted muscles and use those connections in moving, so that you make interesting patterns in space? As you do all these things, you are developing your kinesthetic system, which waits only to be used to become more sensitive. The more you develop your kinesthetic system, the more you will broaden

your capacity to portray various characters. Above all, you will be able to experience and communicate that joy of living which is so important in the drama. The more controlled a body is, the more it seems to be bursting with life. That is why there is so much beauty in a dancer's leap through the air. The reverse is also true: as the body goes out of control, our range of characterization diminishes, and the joy of living leaves us. The less you have developed your kinesthetic system, the less you will enjoy life.

Now consider the closely related balance system. The semicircular canals in your ears tell you when you are properly balanced. If they are damaged, you will feel dizzy all the time. But what they give you is merely information that your body can use in many ways. You can avoid falling by standing with your body straight up and down, but you can also maintain balance in very complicated postures if you keep your center of gravity in the proper place. As you develop your sense of balance, you become better able to judge what kind of movement on one side of your body must be used to compensate for a movement on the other side, so that you will not lose your balance. The better your sense of balance, the more complex the motions you will be able to execute on the stage. A ballet dancer pirouetting on one toe has an extraordinarily well-developed balance system.

A side benefit goes with developing the sense of balance. As you become more sensitive to the internal balance in your body you will also sense balance in the world around you. You will know, for example, much better than you did before, what makes a well-balanced stage picture. As an actor you will work with other actors better to form such a picture. You will understand balance in a larger sense, too—what makes for a well-balanced performance. Is there too much energy expended in the first act, so that the audience is exhausted halfway through the second act? As we begin to sense such connections, we become aware of how closely acting, directing, playwriting, and even producing are related, and how each practitioner benefits from a knowledge of the art of the others.

The third system we are concerned with is the speech-auditory system. The way you speak is related to the way you hear. The speech-auditory system plays a less important role in the development of your personality than the kinesthetic, balance, or visual systems. Consequently it is affected by the other three more than it affects them. Let us see how sound and speech are connected with our kinesthetic activities by considering some examples.

When you listen to music, does it make you want to dance? Do you feel that you can dance well? Does the music form a dance in your mind, even as you sit listening? Or is the music merely a series of sounds that have relatively little meaning for you?

You hear the voice of someone you know in the next room. How do you respond? Do you want to run away? Do you want to hug the person? Do you want to just sit still and play it cool? Can you ever hear a human voice without imagining doing *something* in relation to that voice?

You are speaking. You are addressing a large audience and you have stage fright. Your whole body is shaking, and you want to run away. Doesn't your voice sound as if it, too, wanted to run away? You are furiously angry with someone and you stamp your foot as you shout at him. Doesn't your voice also stamp its foot? Can you ever leave your body completely out of your voice? Perhaps. Sometimes one has to play a disembodied spirit, and the problem is to produce a voice that sounds as if it had no body. It is a strange-sounding voice, to say the least.

Most of the time your voice is so much a part of your body that it cannot help but be affected by what you feel. The people you know well tell you how they feel just by the sounds of their voices. We use the sounds of our voices, sometimes, to exchange feelings with one another. If you are happy and the person you love sounds afraid, you too will be afraid. At the same time, your happy-sounding voice may have begun to reassure him.

We come now to the visual system, which is in many ways the one on which we are most dependent. Vision is a kind of shorthand for experience. If you did not have vision, and you wanted to find out about something, you would have to go up to it and touch it. Once you have learned in infancy to substitute seeing for touching, you can save yourself a lot of steps and learn a great deal more in the same amount of time. Most of what you know about the world you learn through your eyes. You learn to look at things so that you can see how they would feel if you touched them. You thereby make what you see meaningful, for without the imagined feelings you would see only meaningless patches of color and brightness.

No two people see the same way, yet almost everyone assumes that *all* people see the same way. We know that is not true, however, whenever it becomes important to us to know what another person is seeing. How often we hear the remark, "You mean you didn't notice?"

As an actor you must understand and convey what another person sees. You walk into a room, making your entrance. Is it for the first time? What is most striking in the room? What have you, over a lifetime, come to care about that you might find in this room? Perhaps you are a bibliophile, and your whole purpose is to get to the bookcase as quickly as possible and examine the titles. Perhaps you are interested in various kinds of cloth and you are anxious to determine the material of the curtains. If you are a jealous husband, you are looking for clues of a possible lover. If you are a woman in mourning for her husband, you see many things that remind you of the happy years spent with him.

You must also be concerned with the character's general quality of vision. Perhaps he is nearsighted and therefore unaware of anything that is beyond a certain range. Perhaps he has unstable vision and things seem to jump around (for example, if he is intoxicated). In that case, he will have to work hard not to bump into the furniture. Perhaps his vision is very keen and he can memorize the contents of a room at a glance. In that case his eyes may be rather restless and penetrating. Perhaps he sees everything through the romantic haze of being in love. That may give him a languid quality of movement. You must not try to act the symptoms, you must actually *see* what the character sees. Everything else will follow from that.

The way we see affects our posture. The nearsighted man leans forward, peering at everything. His shoulders become hunched, his neck is extended forward, his stomach droops, his spine curves, his feet turn outward. Since he does not see well out of the corners of his eyes, he will regard only what is in front of him, and may often turn his whole body rather than just his head. The person who feels that the world is attacking him may be very stiff. He will sit up rigidly and keep glancing from side to side, always on the lookout for some possible offense. He will be suspicious of anything that is beyond his direct line of vision. That is because what happens in the center of his vision does not seem related to what happens on the periphery. All around him things are going haywire. Under stress he may actually develop tunnel vision so that he will not see out of the corners of his eyes at all.

Some people have very little energy and feel this in their eyes. When they are tired, they often see double. Colors wash out for them. Bright light is painful, and when they are outdoors they often squint. Such a person is likely to look droopy most of the time, as if he feels too tired to stand up. His chest is sunken, his shoulders fall forward, his stomach sticks out.

Most dramatic characters are people of outstanding energy and purpose. The world they see is rich and well organized. Such people have good posture, neither too rigid nor too relaxed, and they exude energy. They are constantly ready for action, constantly full of excitement. Ideally, that should be a sort of basic condition for the actor, as it is far easier for a person with a high energy level to act exhausted than the reverse. Therefore the actor should do his utmost to keep himself in good physical condition generally, and particularly to protect his vision, which is the most sensitive part of his neuromuscular system. He will find that because of the close relationship between the four basic sensory systems, many of the exercises in this book will not only help him feel better and more flexible, but also may help him see better and with greater flexibility. Some things, however, should be done habitually to protect and develop the vision. Let us briefly consider them.

In general, visual performance is dependent upon general physical health. It is extremely important to get enough sleep, to eat the right food, and to keep properly exercised (see Chapter IV). It is also important to avoid specific forms of eyestrain. Since the eyes were developed to focus comfortably at a distance of about twenty feet or more, focusing on anything closer produces some degree of strain. If you are reading or watching television, rest your eyes frequently by staring into space for a few seconds. After half an hour of reading you should exercise mildly for a few minutes. Touching your toes ten times is a good exercise for the purpose. Make certain that you do not read in bed or in a slumped-over position. Have enough light when you are reading. Light should come from behind you, equally distributed on both sides, and be as close as possible to the color of sunlight. You should use illumination that not only lights your book but also lights the rest of the room. If you are watching television, have the room lighted. Focusing on a lighted area surrounded by darkness tends to weaken your periphery so that you cannot see as well out of the corners of your eyes.

Use your eyes as little as possible if you are under physical stress, especially if you have a fever. Remember that the muscles you use for focusing are the most sensitive and easily damaged in your body, and if your other muscles are not functioning properly, it is ridiculous to expect your eye muscles to do so.

On the positive side, you should develop habits of observation and visualization. Play the game "concentration" frequently. Whenever you go into a room for the first time pretend you are going to have to make a drawing of the room when you get home and try to observe and remember everything in it. Notice the expressions on people's faces and try to imagine how they feel inside. Pay particular attention to objects in motion, and try to observe the patterns of motion. Whenever you are reading, try to visualize as fully as possible what you are reading about. Concentrate on getting the picture in your mind as detailed and colorful as possible. Practice looking at things that are in one state or condition and imagining them in another. Imagine how a particular room would look with no furniture in it, or with different furniture, or with the furniture moved around. Imagine how a particular person will look in twenty years, or how he looked twenty years ago. Look at the clouds in the sky and imagine what they represent. Look at abstract paintings and interpret the meaning and feeling they contain. Look at portraits of people and try to imagine those people in other situations, and to determine their characters.

Along with visual development must come development of the other sensory systems. Since none of the systems works alone, one must also be concerned with developing the relationships between them. The best exercise is the one that brings the greatest number of sensory systems into play. In order to understand how this works and why it is so, let us briefly consider the concept of *synesthesia*.

"Tender is the night . . . but here there is no light, save what from heaven is with the breezes blown." These phrases of John Keats are examples of synesthesia. Night, which is ordinarily a visual phenomenon, is given a tactile adjective. The light is imagined to have weight so that it can be blown by the breezes. What is reported by one sense is imagined in terms of another sense. The brain is so organized that our various senses interrelate. Look at a certain color of pink and you can see the sugary taste it has. Listen to a trumpet and then a cello. They call to mind quite contrasting colors and textures. Smell the spring air and it makes your muscles come to life.

To allow the senses to influence one another is desirable because it enormously enriches our awareness. Although we experience a certain amount of synesthesia naturally, we can increase our experience of it by training ourselves to think in terms of it. Here is one exercise that demonstrates how such a thing can happen.

We speak of sounds as being high or low in pitch. It is as if they varied spatially on a vertical plane. As we speak, our voices vary in pitch. We can learn to "see" the variation. Record a sentence on tape, and then listen to it several times, becoming familiar with the inflection pattern. Now try to draw the pattern by making a wavy line that goes up and down just as the voice does. Listen to the recording some more and try to improve your drawing. After you have had some experience, attempt to vary your voice in response to a wavy line that you have already drawn. Next attempt to relate a sound pattern to a movement pattern by suggesting with a dance the inflections that you have heard and produced. As you work with this exercise you will train your ear to become more sensitive to inflection patterns. It is by translating the auditory experience into a visual one that it becomes possible to listen more intelligently. Incidentally, there is nothing new about this exercise. You are working with a primitive system of musical notation.

We shall deal later with more exercises that are designed to develop various forms of synesthesia. Throughout this book we shall be concerned with ways of bringing the various systems in the body into relationship with one another so that the body becomes a highly efficient instrument of communication. Increasingly you will learn to relate the manner of your gesture to the sound of your voice, the way you are standing to the way you are feeling, the quality of your posture to the quality of your mind. As you become more aware of those things, you will begin to see how the finest actors use them in subtle ways to make us feel things about a character the source of which we never quite know.

Chapter II

MOVEMENT AS COMMUNICATION

Everyone has what is called "preferred" posture. That means that when he stands in a relaxed position he will tend to hold his body in a certain way. A surprising number of our impressions of another person stem from our unconscious judgment of his preferred posture. Therefore, as you begin to create a character, you will find it enormously effective to experiment with various postures that might be associated with that character. If you become aware of how you feel in various postures, you will be better able to associate the physical side of the character with his emotional side.

Let us make clearer what we mean by posture. We have all learned that it is a good idea to stand up straight with the shoulders back, the chin up, the chest out, and the stomach in. We therefore tend to associate posture only with those parts of the body, and we tend to think that a person has either good or poor posture. Actually, the variety of postures is infinite, as you will see as soon as you begin to examine people closely. What does a person convey by tilting his head slightly to one side, bringing up the shoulder on that side, and making sure that the chest protrudes? What does he do by having a greater distance between rib and hip on one side than on the other? Most people favor one side of their bodies, so that one shoulder is a little higher, one foot a little straighter, one side carried a little farther forward. Some people mix these things

and stand in very unusual contortions that are difficult to imitate.

All differences in posture, however slight, contribute to the basic impression a person makes on others. As these things are too subtle to be generalized about effectively, they must simply be observed. In Figure 1 the artist has attempted to suggest some of the typical postures that might be observed at a cocktail party. Study the drawing, paying close attention to the many ways in which various postural contortions seem to suggest character. See if you can suggest some of those same character qualities by distorting your own posture. Then, to develop the concept on a more subtle plane, try imitating the postures of various people you know. Observe yourself closely in the mirror until you become well acquainted with your own preferred posture. You might even make a list of the characteristics of your posture as you observe them and compare that list with someone else's impression of you. Knowing your own body will help you to observe other people's bodies sensitively.

We begin our discussion of movement with posture because preferred posture determines the quality of movement that characterizes a person. Gradually, through observation, you must develop a sense of the relationship between movement and posture in each body. Let us now turn our attention to some of the elements of movement in order to help you know what to look for. For pur-

Figure 1

poses of observation we should begin with the movement that characterizes people in normal conversation. After we have built up a sense of character from that situation, we can begin imagining how that type of movement would be extended in other situations.

Consciousness of Motivation

Every gesture is motivated, but since most gestures are habitual, much of the motivation is unconscious. As motivation becomes more conscious, the style of gesture will change. In general, the more conscious the motivation, the more purposeful the gesture.

Contradictoriness of Speech

Some gestures and other bodily movements in effect contradict the words the speaker is uttering. If a person says, "I'm glad to see you," and his body communicates aloofness, then his movement contradicts his words.

Tempo

Movements may be fast or slow, or they may change their tempo while in progress. Rapid movements draw attention to themselves, and often threaten. Slower movements are usually more reassuring.

Rhythm

The general rhythm of a person's life is reflected in all his movements. A person changes his rhythm, however, depending on how he feels and what his situation is. Some gestures are obviously rhythmic, such as tapping one's foot or snapping one's fingers. Most movements are more irregular, and one must observe a person closely for a while before beginning to sense his rhythm.

Length of Pauses

This is really a facet of rhythm, but it can be observed separately. If a person makes no movement for a fairly long time, his inaction may seem threatening to whoever is talking to him. If the pauses between movements are always extremely short, the effect is to make a companion feel either exhilarated or exhausted. When two people are together, the one who feels himself to be inferior will tend to imitate the behavior of the other with regard to such pauses.

Repetitiveness

Some people have quite a limited vocabulary of movement. Their gestures, their mannerisms, are frequently repeated. On the other hand, it may be a special situation that calls forth repetitive movement. A character suffering from shock might repeat the same actions many times.

Interrelatedness

The whole body may work together, or various parts of it may work against one another. A particular gesture may be supported by the whole body, another may seem accidental and irrelevant to the rest of what is happening.

Angularity

Gestures may be rounded or angular. The limbs may be held so that they form sharp angles. The angles may be attractive, or they may make the body seem poorly coordinated.

Differentiation

Gestures may be very efficient, so that only that part of the body needed for expressive purposes will be used. Or they may be so inefficient that a small gesture may never be made because a large part of the body is always involved. The more clearly the parts of the body have been differentiated from one another, the more articulate one's motion can be.

Balance

As he moves, a person may always seem in proper balance, or he may be constantly threatening to lose his balance. Some people cannot stand still for long without shifting their weight. Others stand comfortably and easily in a single position.

Grace

The overall quality of movement may convey a sense of beauty. Some people are always beautiful to watch as they move; others move only awkwardly.

Rigidity

A person may move only with difficulty. He is stiff and rigid, either because his muscles do not operate comfortably, or because psychologically he feels under attack and does not wish to draw attention to himself by excessive motion.

Distance of Exploration

Gestures explore the space around the body. People vary in how far they are willing to extend their arms. Some keep them always quite close to the body. Others frequently reach out almost to arm's length.

Height of Exploration

Some people's gestures never extend above the shoulders or below the waist. Others extend their arms as high or as low as they will go.

Symbolism

Some people often make use of "pictorial" gestures. Others almost never use them. This is conscious symbolism. Unconscious symbolism may include such things as an apparent washing of the hands or frequent clenching of the fist. Most gestures are expressive, rather than symbolic. They are an outlet for the energy of the speaker rather than a repetition of his meaning.

Finger Behavior

The amount of action in the fingers as compared with the whole hand or the arm is significant. Some people almost never move their fingers in gesturing. Others have fingers that are fascinating to watch, that seem almost to be playing a musical instrument.

Forcefulness

How much body energy is behind the gesture? Does it suggest that the speaker is committed to what he is saying, or does it seem weak and helpless?

Weightiness

A gesture may appear weighty without being forceful. Some gestures that are slow-moving and placed rather low suggest the weightiness and dignity of the speaker.

Side Orientation

A person will sometimes orient his movement largely toward one side of his body, almost as if the other side were partially paralyzed. Or he may shift sides but rarely use the central area. Some people avoid the sides and keep their action oriented toward their front. When they turn, they turn the whole body at once.

Protectiveness

Gestures may be used to indicate a kind of defensiveness and insecurity. Like a boxer covering the center of his body, a person may communicate by his movement that he does not wish to leave himself open for attack.

Choppiness

Motion may come in sudden starts and stops rather than flow evenly.

Distractiveness

Some motions distract from what a person is saying. Such a person may be suffering from insecurity and not wish people to attend too closely to what he is saying. Or he may be indicating a lack of concern for other people's interest in him.

Taboo Orientation

Common in Westerns is the action of drinking a beer and then wiping the foam from the mouth with the back of the hand. Many would consider this vulgar, and for them it would be a taboo gesture. People communicate as much by the types of gesture they avoid as by those they indulge in.

Group Identification

Certain types of gesture are adopted by certain groups of people, and use of them reflects an individual's identification with the group. The sophisticated woman holding her cigarette between two carefully angled fingers identifies herself with the Social Register. Less easily described but highly articulate are the characteristic physical behavior patterns of hippies or some blacks.

Use of Props

The cigarette or the wine glass gives some people so much confidence that they even like to be photographed with them. Other common props include eyeglasses, writing implements, handkerchiefs, and fans. Holding something around which he can organize his movement may help a person stylize that movement in a way that pleases him. By his very preference for such a prop, a person indicates his need to structure his personality in relating to others.

Other-Person Orientation

Gesture is a primary means of showing how much one wishes to involve the other person in what one is saying. Leaning toward the other person, touching him from time to time, and gesturing toward him are ways of making him feel that he is really a part of what is being said.

Self-Orientation

The closer one comes to a fetal position, the more one seems to be drawn into oneself. Sitting, with the hands covering the face, is a common way of expressing this. Looking down at one's hands and fidgeting, rather than at the other person, says that one is concentrating on his own thoughts. If the palms of the hands are facing the other person, this expresses an orientation toward him. If they are facing oneself, it expresses the opposite. If they are facing each other, the feeling is neutral, and suggests an emphasis on the situation rather than on either person in the conversation.

Arm and Leg Relationship

In general, it seems natural for a leg to point in the same direction in which an equivalent arm is pointing. If the arms and legs are pointed in different directions, or seem to be operating at odds with one another, the effect is of a person who is confused and perhaps somewhat purposeless.

Trunk Involvement

Sometimes the arms and legs seem to operate as if they were independent of the body, which does not respond at all to what they are doing. The effect is of one who is stiff, or at least hesitant and lacking in conviction. In a livelier person, the trunk provides a background for any action of the arms and legs. If this tendency is carried to extremes, however, the effect is that the arms and legs do not have their own purposes, and that the individual is always totally immersed in any action in which he is involved and therefore incapable of considering other possibilities at the same time.

Head Involvement

The head normally relates to what the rest of the body is doing. If there is no head involvement, other movement will seem stilted and even meaningless. The primary reflection of emotion is in the face, and the rest of the body underlines and emphasizes what the face is saying. If the head moves too much compared to the rest of the body, it seems to substitute for it, and the effect is of superficiality in whatever is being expressed. In other words, the body is used to give depth to whatever the face expresses.

Masking Tendencies

Parts of the body may be used to conceal other parts. A person who has just had his teeth removed may keep one hand in such a position that it covers his mouth. Keeping the arms folded across the chest has the effect, sometimes, of masking part of the body. Keeping the head down conceals the face to some degree. The more insecure a person is, the more he will tend to mask parts of his body in any way that he can.

Tension

Movement always reveals the degree of tension in the body. If there is too much tension, gestures will be uncontrolled, perhaps so much so that the limbs are trembling. As tension reduces, movement becomes easier and either more relaxed or more graceful. Too little tension makes a person appear dull and sleepy. The actor uses certain kinds of tension purposely to help him project what his body is saying.

We have considered some of the various types of movement. You can easily observe many others. As you become sensitive to how typical movement varies from person to person, you will become better able to characterize through gesture and motion.

We should observe, however, that there is an important difference between the kind of movement that characterizes an individual in real life and that which is appropriately used on the stage. All art selects and abstracts from life. That is particularly true in the art of stage movement. In order that the movement used to characterize may be clear to an audience at some distance, it must be *exaggerated*. In order that it may say exactly what needs to be said artistically, no more and no less, it must be *selected* from the total complexity of real life. In order that it may relate to other movements that come before and after it, it must be *organized* more carefully and consciously than real life movement. In order for it to say something about the human condition in general, rather than just a single person, it must be *abstracted* to some degree. Let us briefly discuss each concept in turn.

Exaggeration does not simply mean making things bigger. In fact, a gesture on the stage may be no larger than the equivalent gesture in real life would be. But the stage gesture is more definite, more purposeful, more clearly stated, more precise. Even the most naturalistic style of acting necessarily exaggerates. For example, scratching one's nose should be done in such a way that it says, "Look at me; I am scratching my nose; I am the type of person who scratches his nose in a situation like this; pay attention to my particular kind of sloppiness."

Selection means using only those gestures which add to character and clarify it. None of the nervous mannerisms of the actor must be allowed to interfere. The body may be allowed to contradict itself only to express the confusion of the character. The focus must always be so designed that the audience understands what a particular action is trying to communicate.

Organization means thinking of movement in terms of patterns that are cumulative. Once a particular gesture has been used, it may be unnecessary to use it again. Stage movement should increase in dramatic intensity. The most surprising, dramatic things that are going to be said about a character in terms of movement must be saved until near the end of his part. Sometimes, however, a particular style of entrance may be used to tell us immediately what to expect from a character throughout a scene. For example, a fop may enter with an elaborate bow, which he then continues to use during the scene. In such a case, movements become subtle variations on a clearly stated theme.

Abstraction is used to make us feel that something basic in human nature is revealed by the actions selected. We must know, through behavior, not only the individual, but the type of character represented. Type may include such concepts as nationality (a particular style of walking is associated with the characters in *The Mikado*), occupation (military figures may be immediately identified by their stance), class (the beggar has a characteristic slouch), general attitude (the angry young man has an aggressive manner), and station in life (the aging matron is not difficult to distinguish from the sweet young thing). It may also include behavior patterns that transcend the other kinds of groups (Lucy in *Peanuts* has some of Bottom the Weaver in her).

In general, the actor should use about as much abstraction in physical characterization as the playwright has used in verbal characterization. Thus, one style is appropriate to the heroic characters of Shakespeare, another for the realistic characters of Tennessee Williams, and yet another for the abstract characters of Eugène Ionesco. As the style of the playwright moves away from realism, the style of the actor should move in the direction of dance.

As soon as the actor accepts the fact that while he is onstage everything about his appearance in motion will be interpreted by the audience, he will see the need to develop the kind of artistic intelligence that observes widely, remembers in depth, and uses only the best of what has been remembered.

Chapter III

EXPLORING THROUGH EXERCISE

Many people dislike exercise. Typical of their attitude is the famous quip, "Whenever I get an impulse to exercise, I lie down until it goes away." Exercise is thought of as painful, boring, time-consuming, and in some tedious way "good for you." It can be all of those things, but it can also be an exciting means of discovery.

We would all like to be able to realize that dream of glory in which one is suddenly discovered to be a great actor, a great musician, or a great painter. The dream is fed by the knowledge that a few people in history have achieved artistic greatness seemingly without effort. Mozart was able to learn to play the violin simply by watching someone else do so for about fifteen minutes. Those of us who do not have such gifts are forced to develop our ability slowly through regular exercise of a kind appropriate to the ability we are trying to develop.

The exercises suggested in this book are all means of exploring one's body in order to learn the art of acting. If they are done properly, they should ultimately produce more pleasure than pain, more excitement than tedium, more freshness than repetition. But that will not necessarily be so at first. It may help you, however, if we explain at this point an attitude toward exercise that will make it produce results more quickly. Exercise can benefit you much more if you are thinking about it as you do it.

Your objective is to produce movements that communicate artistically. In order to do so you must get to know your interior as a means of controlling your exterior. Every individual motion that you make has a feeling that is unique. You will perceive the uniqueness of the feeling only if you are looking for it. In time you will become increasingly able to relate the feeling that occurs inside your body to a sense of how your moving body appears to others at a distance.

You must concentrate on getting to know all the muscles in your body and how they interrelate, not by studying them in a textbook, but by feeling them as you exercise them. You will be concerned with sensing your muscles in two ways. First, you must sense the relationship between how your muscle feels inside and how it looks to an observer. Second, you must sense how your body as a totality is relating to space as you move through space.

Let us consider how one gets started on sensing the relationship between the way a muscle feels and the way it looks. Try looking at your hand in the manner suggested by Figure 2. Long ago you differentiated the various parts of your hand by looking at them and giving them names. You also differentiated them by associating certain kinesthetic sensations with each part. As you are looking at your hand, try to associate the kinesthetic sensation with the visual impression of each of the parts that are named. You must learn to make such associations between kinesthesia and sight if you are to sense how your body looks as it moves. In other words, your kinesthetic impressions must conjure up visual images so that you will know how you appear to others.

Next consider how one may explore the body with a view to discovering its changing relationships as it moves through space. Let us approach the problem by making an

find a painting or a reproduction and study it for several minutes. Try to keep your mind actively involved as you look at it. You are hunting for new details. You are also trying to see why the artist put the details together as he did. See how long you can continue seeing new things in the painting, how deeply you can develop your interest in it.

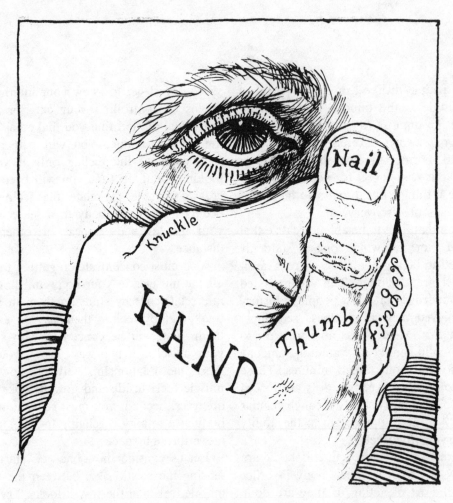

Figure 2

analogy. As you look at a painting for the first time you get a very general impression of its subject matter and color scheme. A great many details escape your notice. There are also organizational principles of which you are not aware. Study the painting carefully for a while, and you will see more of the details, and also how the details interrelate. Before reading further in this book,

After you have studied the painting, see if you can look at your own body with the same kind of intellectual involvement as you study it from the inside. Bend over and touch your toes. Hold that position, and while you are holding it, explore your body with your mind. You will notice first the muscles in your back and legs that are being stretched. Think about them carefully. Where are they situated in your body? Can you visualize them well enough to make a rough drawing of them? Are there muscles immediately surrounding them that remain relaxed? After you have explored the muscles that force themselves upon your attention because of the pain you feel in them, begin to explore others as well. Become aware of your toes, your neck, your shoulders, your elbows, and so on. Let your mind roam around in your body, exploring here and there at random, returning to places of special interest. You are looking at some of the details of your body structure.

Next begin to explore the structure itself. How are your toes connected to your feet, your feet to your ankles, and so on? You might run through the song "Dry Bones," thinking about each part of your body as it comes up in the song. Develop a sense of how your body is connected, one part to the next.

But the connections that are determined by proximity are not the only kind of connections you need to explore. Much more important are the connections that are formed in the mind between muscles in widely separate parts of the body. You can build a connection between any two parts of you that you wish merely by thinking about it. How, for example, do your toes relate to your shoulders? How does your jaw relate to your left hip? How does your nose relate to your knees?

All such exploration can happen without any motion in the body and with the eyes closed, merely by thinking about the connections that are possible, merely by focusing one's attention on various parts of one's body. The next step is to consider the body in motion. Let us begin with a very simple motion.

Shift your weight from side to side so that you slowly sway from left to right and back again. Begin by doing this with the feet, so that the whole body is in motion. Then sway from the hips. Finally, use the shoulders. Notice how the sensations in your body

differ with each of the motions. Explore the sensations of motion exactly as you did the sensations of the body at rest. Think about the connections between the various parts of your body and how they change as the body moves. You will come to realize that any motion affects many parts of the body differently. You will also discover that the quality of motion can be changed. One becomes gradually more precise in making each of the three movements described as he practices it. Try to become aware enough of your body so that you know that each time you sway you are doing so a little differently.

Next, consider the problem of discovering in how many parts of the body one can originate the swaying motion. You have tried three. Perhaps you think you could find about three more. Actually, if you study the problem carefully for a while, you should become aware that there are probably as many as a hundred positions from which the swaying may originate. Many of them would become possible only after a great deal of practice, but you should be able to think about them even if you cannot do them.

Perhaps you can see that if one takes the proper attitude he can turn the very simplest physical exercise into an exciting intellectual challenge, and, what is more, begin to do so the first time he encounters the exercise. It requires mental discipline to keep one's mind working in this way, of course, but the more one does so the more rapidly the exercises will begin to take effect.

We have considered so far only the way one explores one's body from the inside. Let us examine how one exercises with a view toward imagining the forms he is creating in space. Again, it may help to deal first with an analogy.

If you are reading an exciting book and enjoying the experience, you are visualizing as you read. Words are transformed into images, and the images move through your mind much as a film or a television program moves on the screen. In other words, as you read about something you dramatize it in your head. The capacity of the mind to visualize thus is important, and is too little used.

We are going to ask you to learn to apply the same visualization process to the behavior of your own body. As you perform, you create a second self who sits in the audience and watches the performance (Figure 3). You adjust your performance to satisfy the critical eye of this second self.

Go back, now, to touching your toes. You are bent over, and you are imagining how you look bent over. You should have a fairly good idea of how you look when you are standing up, as you are used to seeing people in that position, and in general you look as other people do. You are less used to seeing people bent over. You are going to try to work out logically how you look while you are bent over. Close your eyes and imagine yourself standing upright. Then imagine yourself touching your toes. Touch your toes in your imagination ten times without actually moving. Do you seem to retain a consistent height, or does the size of your body seem to change?

You should begin to relate the feeling of the muscles in your back and legs to a sense of the reduction of your height. You should also think about the greater depth in your body as a result of your doubling over. Concentrate on visualizing the distances.

Next work with a mirror. Standing before the mirror, touch your toes and imagine standing up. Then actually stand up and compare the image in your mind with the image in the mirror. Repeat the process several times and become more critical of the image in your mind. Do the same thing standing sideways in front of the mirror, so that you can check your visualization of the depth of your body with the image in the mirror.

So far we have been working with kinesthesia as a basis for imagery. In the following exercise, we shall reverse the process. You are to stand facing another person and create a mirror image of that person's actions. Here you are moving from the image to the action. Inasmuch as the image originates outside of you, the action will feel somewhat strange until you get used to the process. At the same time you will be learning to match an image with an action.

Finally, work with some of the photographs in this book. Select a picture and attempt to imitate the posture that it represents. Get into your body what you feel to be the most accurate imitation of the picture you are capable of, then check yourself in the mirror. Make the necessary corrections. Then walk around the room a few times in order to get the sensations associated with the action out of your body and then try the same thing again. You will probably find that it continues to be necessary to make corrections even though you are sure you have reproduced the photograph accurately.

As an extension of this exercise, get the feeling the photograph represents into your body, and then create a series of movements that follow logically from that feeling. If this makes no sense to you, or if you feel that the movements you create are more or less arbitrary, that is a sign that you need to work much harder to understand the meaning of the movement in relation to the feeling in your body.

If you practice thinking about exercise as you do it, you will begin to discover the immense complexity of the human body and its tremendous capacity for expressiveness. A time will come when you can apply the thinking that you do about your own exercising to your observation of other people. It will be increasingly easy for you to empathize with various physical states. That is the first step in learning to imitate the actions of others as a basis for creating character. You will know that you have reached your objective when you find yourself able to stand upon the stage acting for a second self who then gives you instructions as to how to change your movements in order to produce the results he has in mind. You will

Figure 3

have learned to combine in yourself the simultaneous roles of actor and director.

As you work through the exercises in this book, you will notice that many of them are usually associated with the training of dancers. A strong feeling exists among some students of dance and of drama that no attempt should be made to combine the two media. That is because drama is primarily representational, whereas dance is primarily abstract. Whether or not the two can be effectively combined depends more on the inspiration of creative genius than on pre-ordained laws of the performing arts. Our present concern, however, is the development of flexibility in performance, and this is achieved through the use of many exercises that apply only indirectly to situations that might be performed. The area of concern common to the actor and the dancer is the development of a full understanding of one's own body. The conditioning of it, exploration in space with it, and meaningful use of it are vital to the success of either. Thus, much of what the actor must do to grow more acquainted with his body is exactly what the dancer must do. Most of the basic exercises are the same, and many of the improvisational sketches are useful to both. We have given some consideration to the ways that functional movement influences the dancer and abstract movement influences the actor. Those who combine an interest in drama with an interest in dance will be pleased to learn how much they have in common. Those who do not may find an additional interest developing. It is even possible that you will consider ways in which drama and dance can be combined to form an entirely new art, taking nothing away from the singularity of each as a separate art form.

We are ready now to consider specific exercises designed to develop specific skills. They are to some extent arranged in an order that should help you to grow as a performer. It is probable that you will find some of them much easier than others. If you will concentrate on those areas that are most difficult, you should be able to use this book to build for yourself an individual program of exercise designed to broaden your range and depth as a performing artist.

PART II—BUILDING A FOUNDATION

Chapter IV

GIVING YOUR BODY ITS DUE

Your body is a system that functions with varying degrees of efficiency. It is so designed that when it is under stress it learns to work around the stress. For example, if you break your right arm it will not be long before you feel relatively comfortable doing many things with your left hand that it has never done before. Your body adapts to the stress of the broken arm by working around it.

But there is a catch. Every time the body adapts to stress it functions a little less efficiently. That means that if you are under stress you may learn to ignore the stress to the extent that you no longer believe it exists, but you will find it a little more difficult to do everything that you normally do. Your overall performance will drop: You will get fewer things done, you will do each thing less well, you will get tired more quickly, you will be more irritable, and so on. Therefore, all other things being equal, it is always desirable to reduce stress in the body.

What is stress? There are many kinds of stress, but in general, stress is anything that makes it more difficult for your body to operate as a biological and psychological organism (Figure 4). Among the most common forms of stress are: inadequate nutrition, inadequate sleep, inadequate exercise, excessive food, excessive exercise, physical damage through accident, use of drugs of all kinds, eyestrain, disease, depression, noise, pollution, anxiety, and environmental unpredictability. We are all exposed to all of these things some of the time, so stress in rather large amounts is a universal part of human experience. Every time you reduce stress or avoid it, you give yourself a chance to function more efficiently than you otherwise would. One of your objectives, therefore, should be to reduce stress in your life in as many ways as possible.

If you have already had some experience in the theatre, it is probable that you have sometimes found rehearsals fatiguing. When you are fatigued during a rehearsal, the quality of performance that you can eventually achieve in that production is somewhat reduced, because you will not get as much out of the rehearsal as you otherwise would. You can reduce the tendency to feel fatigued much of the time, and consequently increase the overall quality of your performances, by doing primarily three things:

First, make sure that you are getting adequate nutrition. If you are between the ages of 13 and 20, you are growing very rapidly. The rapid growth is itself a source of stress. The quality of the food you eat will have a tremendous impact on how you feel at any time of your life, but particularly during those years. Nationwide studies indicate that teen-agers almost invariably receive poor nutrition. If you skip breakfast, eat a peanut butter sandwich for lunch, stock up on soft drinks and candy bars in the afternoon, and make dinner your main meal, you are receiving very poor nutrition and putting yourself automatically under tremen-

Figure 4

dous avoidable stress. If you are a girl who is worried about her figure and often goes on crash diets, you may be doing permanent harm not only to your own body but also to the bodies of the children you may someday have. For information about proper nutrition, read a book such as *Let's Eat Right to Keep Fit* by Adelle Davis (see Bibliography).

In connection with nutrition, it is necessary to observe that many things you put in your body may have an effect on your total personality. Because of the complexity of the human body it is difficult to know exactly what that effect is. The chemistry of your body may react in one of at least three ways to anything that is not good for it. It may respond directly with symptoms of disaster, as it does to poisons. Thus, you may vomit or break out in a rash or feel dizzy as a result of eating something that is not good for you. It may respond indirectly, with side effects. Thus, a drug that is used to save your life by killing a virus may make your hair fall out. Or it may respond gradually over a long period of time. Thus, you may spend forty years building up to a heart attack or to lung cancer. No two bodies react in exactly the same way to all chemical substances, and it is therefore difficult to predict exactly what will happen to a person as a result of taking anything into his body. In general, however, foods have a more beneficial effect on the body than drugs. Even aspirin, taken to cure a headache, can seriously deplete your body's supply of vitamin C and thus make you more susceptible to catching a cold.

At the present time there is considerable controversy about the advantages and disadvantages of taking drugs, particularly drugs that have a pronounced effect on the functioning of the mind. We shall not here discuss the moral or the legal problems associated with drugs, but you should know something about the physiological problems you may experience as a result of taking them. Remember that any drug, whether aspirin, nicotine, alcohol, marijuana, or LSD, places the body under some stress. Bodies react differently, but all experience *some* stress. If you are a regular user of a drug and you also feel fatigued much of the time, it may be that your fatigue is partly caused by use of the drug. If that is so, no amount of improvement in your nutrition, exercise, and sleep will completely eliminate the fatigue, and you should consider reducing or eliminating your use of the drug. That applies as much to caffeine as it does to marijuana, as much to alcohol as it does to LSD, and as much to nicotine as it does to Dexedrine.

A feeling of dependence on any drug is relatively difficult to overcome, and it is sometimes true that the stress of doing without the drug is in certain respects greater than the stress caused by the drug. In evaluating your own relation to this statement, bear in mind that it is just that—*your* relation to it. If you are surrounded by people who smoke, that does not reduce the effect of smoking on your body. To the extent that you want to do your best as a performing artist, you will have to come to terms with your body chemistry.

The above statements may sound puritanical, particularly in the light of the fact that most famous actors are regular users of some kind of drug. Again, we return to the fact that you must evaluate your relationship to yourself, not to anyone else. The fact that a famous movie star smokes has no bearing on whether you should smoke. We are also being practical rather than moralistic. We are concerned with how you can get the most from your body. Obviously you will cut corners in some areas and make your own decisions about how much you wish to attempt to achieve. Keep in mind that one of the factors affecting your decision should be a practical concern for your overall physical and mental efficiency and those things that affect it.

The next important factor in maintaining physical stamina is the amount of exercise you get. If you fall below a certain minimum per week you will feel much more exhausted all of the time than it is ever necessary for you to feel. A book is available that can help you work out an exercise program best suited to your individual situation and needs. It is based on careful scientific study of the exercise requirements of the human body. Read *Aerobics* by Kenneth H. Cooper (see Bibliography). You may also wish to consult the *Royal Canadian Air Force Exercise Plans for Physical Fitness* as a supplement to (though not a substitute for) *Aerobics*.

Many people who devote much of their time to theatre fall into the habit of getting very little sleep. If you are one of those who consistently get three or four hours a night, you need to reconsider what you are doing. It is true that the amount of sleep needed differs with each individual, but most people who live on small amounts of sleep are putting themselves under stress that lowers their overall efficiency. There is a way you can find out how much sleep you actually need in order to operate at your optimum level of efficiency, but it may take you some time to accomplish. When you are eating properly and getting enough exercise (failure to do so will limit your ability to sleep properly), you should set aside several weeks during which you can be relatively relaxed. In doing the following experiment, sleep on a bed with a firm mattress. The firmer your mattress, the more your sleep will rest you. Go to bed fairly early, about 9 or 10 o'clock, and sleep until you feel fully rested and ready to get up and start the day. Do not use an alarm clock, but wake up only when you are ready to. You should sleep in an area in which you will not be awakened too early by the noise of other people in the house or in the neighborhood. You will probably find that the amount of sleep you feel you need varies for a while. You may have trouble sleeping at first, or you may sleep for an unusually long time. After a time you will begin to sleep about the same amount each night. When you have been getting about the same amount of restful sleep each night for about two weeks, you will have determined the approximate amount of sleep your body needs. From that time on you will feel better if you see to it that you always get that amount. It is important to emphasize that although some people may be able to function effectively on two hours or less of sleep out of twenty-four, that does not mean that you can. Do not try to force your body to behave as if it were someone else's. You will pay a tremendous price for doing so. Also, do not fall into the fallacy of believing that sleep is a waste of time. Proper amounts of sleep will save you time because you will accomplish more and find life more enjoyable during your waking hours.

Many people when they are confronted by the above demands respond by saying, "I don't need to do those things. I feel fine the way I'm living now." Such people often go on to admit to emotional problems, irritability, feelings of fatigue, or a belief that they cannot possibly do anything as well as they feel they should. But even if one really does feel good while cheating his body of its biological needs, he should realize that there are relative degrees of feeling good. If you are one of those who can live on coffee and doughnuts, never exercise, and sleep two hours a night and still feel good, why deprive yourself of the joy of feeling absolutely wonderful all the time as a result of giving your body what it needs?

A word of caution: If you have been cheating yourself for a long time and you change your ways, do not expect to feel good all at once. Proper nutrition may make you feel sick to your stomach. Proper exercise may make you feel as if you are going to have a heart attack. A good night's sleep may make you feel groggy all the next day. The reason such things occur is that once your body has adapted to stress, it will have to readapt once the stress is removed.

You cannot change yourself too rapidly. You must gradually get used to living properly. It may be several months before you are able to appreciate the benefits of giving your body what it needs. Take heart: When you have made the adjustment you will have achieved something that will make you happier than you can possibly imagine. Once you have learned to live properly, you will never again desire to go back to your old ways.

Chapter V

THE BASIC EXERCISES

In the previous chapter we discussed in general terms stress and its effect on human efficiency. In order to understand the exercises in this chapter, we need to understand a particular kind of stress that we shall call the stress of disorganization.

The more organized you are in approaching any given situation, the more efficiently you will be able to deal with that situation. What is true of you as a total person is also true of your body. Patterns of organization are formed within your body, and the quality of their organization has something to do with your overall efficiency. The most basic exercises are those designed to improve the efficiency of the body as a whole and thereby to make one more responsive to other exercises that have a more specialized effect.

The best of all exercises is *walking,* because it distributes its benefits equally throughout the body. Furthermore, walking can provide a controlled and thoughtful interaction with the environment.

Since it is possible to walk in a manner that disorganizes you and intensifies the stress in your body, let us begin by considering some of the ways in which you should *not* walk. Picture yourself carrying a heavy load of books under one arm while the other swings freely. As you walk, you are looking at the ground in front of your feet. Your whole body is angled so that it tends to hunch around the load you are carrying. One foot drags behind the other with a sort of limp. Your feet hit the ground flatly and lifelessly.

What is wrong with such a way of walking? To understand the difficulty you must realize that the human body is basically symmetrical not only in form but also in operation. You have two arms and two legs, two whole sides of your body, which should as much as possible mirror each other's action. The balance between the two sides is important, and the degree to which it is established has an important effect on how efficiently you operate. If one side of your body tends to drag along after the other side, it is as if you had only half a body; the other half is dead weight. Worse, the two halves may work against each other, creating needless confusion. You want the halves to work together as exactly as possible.

Begin by getting rid of that load of books that is throwing you off balance. If you *must* carry the books, at least divide the load equally between your two hands. Bear in mind, however, that any load you carry is a stress and will tend to throw your body off balance in many ways. Therefore, while you are practicing walking, practice under the best conditions you can arrange, and try to avoid carrying anything.

Next get your eyes off the ground. If you are so unsure of yourself that you will fall down a manhole if you are not looking at the ground all the time, you should not be out walking at all. Keep your gaze fixed straight ahead and look as far into the distance as possible. Your chin should be roughly parallel with the ground. There should be a straight line from the top of your head to the base of your spine. To get that established, you may need to spend some time practicing the following exercise:

Stand with your head, shoulders, and heels against a wall, your chin parallel to the floor. Place a book on the top of your head so that it balances there. Now walk around the room, being careful not to drop the book (Figures 5 and 6). Learn the feeling associated with a straight back and neck. When you are relatively comfortable walking with the book on your head, you are ready to do without it, but you may want to come back to this exercise from time to time to remind yourself how a straight back feels.

As you walk down the road keeping your eyes straight ahead, you want your mind to work on what you are seeing. Alternate between focusing on the most distant point straight ahead of you and trying to be aware of the whole picture that surrounds you. Try to see out of the corners of both eyes simultaneously. If you do this well enough, you may find that things are sharper and clearer when you are focusing straight ahead and that they tend to blur a little when you are concentrating on the whole picture. That is a good sign. It means that you are learning to see more of the world at one time, and that you are temporarily sacrificing a little detail while you are doing so.

Now pay attention to what your arms are doing. They should swing alternately with the action of your legs. The swing of each arm should mirror that of the other. Have someone walk behind you and check whether you are swinging one arm more than the other, or whether the swinging action of your arms tends to veer away from the center of your body. To keep the swing properly centered, let the most forward position of each arm line up exactly with your navel.

You want your chest out rather than sunken as you walk, but there is a way to accomplish this naturally so that it arises out of the total action of your body. You must consolidate the lowest part of your trunk. Press your pubic area inward so that it reaches toward the base of your spine. The resulting tension will be the foundation of a tension that pulls your stomach inward and your chest out.

Now we must consider the action of the hips and the legs. Most people think that in walking one leg is more or less idle while the other is engaged in moving. You should think of both legs as working all the time, so that your weight is constantly being shifted between them. With that in mind, walk in front of a mirror and check the following points:

1. Your toes should be pointed straight ahead at all times.

2. Your feet should be about four inches apart so that they fall directly below your hips.

3. Each leg should swing straight through below the hip and not deviate to either side. You may find that there is a tendency for one or both feet to kick out with each step. This tendency is difficult to control because the action is unconscious, but with patience one can learn to control it.

4. The hip regions should rotate much in the manner of the pedals on a bicycle. This raising and lowering of the hips will make it possible for the leg to swing straight through, as indicated above.

5. Each foot should rise the same distance off the ground, so that one foot is not dragging in comparison with the other.

6. The knees should be flexible enough to lift the legs well off the ground.

Finally, we consider the action of your feet. There should be flexibility in your ankles so that your feet do not seem mere extensions of your legs, but transmit your weight evenly to the ground in their own way. Your foot should come down lightly but firmly on the heel; and as your weight

Figure 5

Figure 6

moves forward it should roll forward onto the ball of the foot, simulating the action of a wheel. As your toes make contact with the ground they should perform a grasping action that will help to push you forward into the next step.

You may find that your toes are not very sensitive to what you are asking them to do. Possibly your feet are so crammed into your shoes that your toes cannot operate freely. If that is so, you may need to change your shoe size. For information on the proper way to get shoes that fit your feet, read *Take Off Your Shoes and Walk* by Simon J. Wikler (see Bibliography).

Our discussion of walking probably makes it seem a far more complex exercise than you had ever thought it could be. No doubt you wonder why it is worth the trouble to walk thus. A number of answers may be given, only some of which we shall have space to consider.

The first point is that walking in the manner we have described is the most effective single means available to you to help the two sides of your body work together effectively. The better they do so, the less stress there will be in the interaction of muscles throughout your body. Changing your way of walking should in time increase the amount of energy available to you in all of the things you do, since decreasing the stress automatically caused by faulty muscular patterns eliminates an important drain on your energy.

The second point is that once you have mastered the kind of walking we have described to the extent that it becomes your natural walk, you will become a more physically attractive person, particularly as seen from a distance. Both your posture and the grace with which you move will be significantly improved, and those two factors are important in determining physical attractiveness. As an actor you will wish to be as attractive as possible in any role that is not specifically characterized as unattractive.

Furthermore, the additional energy you will have as a result of graceful movement will communicate itself to others, increasing your physical attractiveness even more.

The third point is that a graceful walk will help to make you feel more a part of your surroundings as you walk. You will tend to notice what is happening around you more. You will spend less time wrapped up in your own thoughts, more time making the observations that must be the basis of your work as an artist.

The fourth point is that since walking is the kind of exercise you do the most (the average person walks 1,300 miles every year), you can, by changing your walking patterns, build a foundation that will make it easier for you to benefit from all the other exercising you do.

All of the above points have a significant bearing on the quality of your work as an actor. You should consider their implications carefully both now and whenever you are walking. If you will attempt to employ the suggestions we have made for improving your walking, you will soon begin to find that walking is an extraordinarily dynamic process that you can experience in an almost infinite variety of ways. A multitude of insights about the action of your body can occur to you as you are walking, and you can carry those insights over into your work as an actor. In a later chapter we shall discuss various ways of walking in the creation of a character and in the exploration of communicative movements. Improving your personal style of walking will be of enormous help to you in doing those exercises in particular.

Our second basic exercise is *crawling*. Early in your life you did a great deal of crawling, and you have probably not done any since. The crawling stage of life helps to establish basic muscular patterns that govern actions of all sorts. Its importance has become particularly evident to some remedial educators who have found that many learning problems can be corrected by improving basic muscular patterns through practice in crawling.

Since you established your muscular patterns as a child, a great deal has happened to you; and it is unlikely that the crawling you would do now would be similar to the crawling you did then. Like other basic skills, crawling benefits from occasional review.

What is it that you can learn from crawling? You know that your arms and legs work together in many ways. Whether you are riding a bicycle, playing tennis, or dancing, you must coordinate the action of the arms and legs. In acting, coordination is extremely important, as any lack of it will produce an appearance of awkwardness in movement. The four limbs are all connected to one another through the muscles of the back. You probably do not think of your back as a very dynamic part of your body, but it is. Just how dynamic is something that becomes evident as you attempt to crawl. Suddenly your back will come alive as having all the intricacy of a complex telephone system, but one that you will soon discover is rather rusty through lack of use.

In order to make crawling comfortable, you will probably want to purchase a pair of knee pads, available at most drugstores. You will also want to do your crawling on a mat or a thick rug if possible. You will probably find the exercise rather tiring at first, as you will be using muscles in unaccustomed ways, and it is therefore important to do a little each day and gradually build up your tolerance. At first you may find that five minutes is all you can handle.

The most obvious way to crawl is that used by babies. The right hand moves as the left leg does, and vice versa. Practice this technique for a while and get used to the idea of crawling before you begin to refine the exercise by adding other techniques.

The first variation is to move both limbs on each side of you at the same time. You will find this variation awkward at first, com-

pared to the technique you are more used to. Therefore, practice it separately for a while. When you have become equally comfortable with both techniques, alternate between them at increasingly short intervals.

You can further refine the exercise by realizing that when two limbs are moving together you have several choices of timing. You can raise the arm, then the leg, then lower the arm and then the leg. You can raise and lower both simultaneously. You can raise and lower the leg before the arm. You can raise the leg first and lower it last, or raise the arm first and lower it last. Practice all the variations and you will find that you have learned ten ways of crawling.

So far, as you have crawled, your arms and legs have supported your trunk in the air. Your trunk therefore plays a relatively passive role, simply following the motion of the limbs. Now lower the trunk onto the floor so that it must do its own moving, inching its way along in relation to the movement of the limbs. Try all ten of the variations in that position. You will then find that you have learned twenty ways of crawling.

We add twenty more simply by turning over and facing the back to the floor. Forty crawling techniques can thus be learned if you are willing to take the time to do so. As a child, you probably used only one of them. Learn the forty techniques and you will be amazed at the subtlety of the interrelationships you can discover between the various parts of your body. If you study crawling alone and no other exercise in this book, it should become possible for you to increase the subtlety and variety of your acting so much that you will scarcely recognize the actor you once were.

Let us turn our attention now to the problem of *balance*. We have all witnessed many times the nervous person who stands before a group and continually shifts his weight from one leg to the other. Sometimes the habit is so distracting that we become more fascinated with watching his movement than with listening to what he has to say. People who behave in this way (and most people who have not been taught otherwise *do* behave in this way) have relatively poor control over their ability to distribute their weight equally between both legs. You will find that your balance becomes crucial when you have to perform complex actions on the stage, such as fencing or walking rapidly down a flight of stairs or dancing. The better your sense of balance, the more control you will have over every action you perform.

Two devices you can construct for yourself are most useful in developing the sense of balance. They are the *walking rail* and the *balance board*. To make a walking rail all you need is a number of blocks about the size of bricks and a set of long boards of varying widths. The idea is to build a rail above the ground so that one has to maintain balance in order to walk on it. As a result of the varying widths of the boards, the walk along the rail should vary in difficulty as you proceed, so that sometimes you find it difficult not to fall off, whereas at other times you can concentrate on walking as smoothly and naturally as possible. You will develop your sense of balance not only by not falling off the boards, but also by learning to adjust to the various widths of the boards.

The balance board (Figure 7) is constructed from a piece of plywood having an area 1' x 1' and two square blocks of different widths but thicknesses of about 2". Center the blocks one on each side of the plywood square and nail them in place. One of the blocks should be of such a size that when you attempt to balance on it you can do so with relative ease, provided you are thinking about balancing. The other, smaller one should be of a size that makes it difficult but not impossible for you to maintain balance. Thus by turning the board over you move from an easy to a difficult balancing problem.

You will use the balance board in the following way. Stand on the easy side of it and recite a dramatic speech. Each time the board tips you must go back and start the speech over. When you can get through the speech easily without tipping the board you will have discovered a certain feeling of equilibrium. Memorize that feeling. Now turn the board over and repeat the process. Try to establish the same feeling of equilibrium you had on the other side. From time to time reverse the board to refresh your memory as to what is required. When the difficult side of the board has become easy for you, you are ready to build yourself a new balance board in order to take an additional step in refining your sense of balance.

From time to time when you are not using the balance board, pretend that you are, and try to conjure up the feeling of hard-won equilibrium you associate with it. Eventually you should have that feeling automatically whenever you are acting.

As practice improves your sense of balance, you should find it easier to handle acting situations that you previously found difficult. Some of these situations will be purely physical ones of the sort we previously described. Some of them will be psychological, because as the amount of energy you unconsciously use to maintain your balance decreases, the amount of concentration you can put into other activities increases. Thus you will be able to think through acting situations that previously seemed too difficult, and to add subtlety and control to your acting style.

Another way of improving your sense of balance is to practice *hopping*. Learn to hop in patterns. Hop twice on the right foot, three times on the left, five times on the right, once on the left and so on, according to a predetermined series of numbers. Hop different distance intervals. Hop backwards. Hop in circles, squares, and other patterns. You can develop your own hopping exercises easily, making sure that each exercise sets you a goal that you can reach only with concentration. As you become a better hopper, set more complex goals for yourself. Get

Figure 7

good enough at hopping so that you can hop in time to complex rhythmic patterns.

Still another balance exercise is the following walking technique. You must have your shoes off for this one. Curl your toes under your feet as far as they will go. Keeping them curled, walk, placing your feet one directly in front of the other. Most of your weight will be on the sides of your feet. Try to distribute it equally throughout the feet, walking *very* slowly in order to achieve this. You will find that it is difficult to keep your balance while doing this, but that you will be able to make subtle refinements in posture that help you to get your sense of balance under control.

A fourth basic exercise is *movement pattern memorization*. You will need to do this with someone else. The leader performs a simple pattern with the feet, such as a box step. The follower imitates it. The leader continues to perform more complex patterns until the follower has difficulty remembering what he has done. They remain at that level until the follower finds he can remember easily what the leader does. Then the leader initiates more complex steps. If the follower can remember accurately what the leader has done 75 percent of the time, it is time to move to a more complex level. When complicated foot patterns have been mastered, complexity is then increased by introducing simultaneous arm and leg movements. The goal is to imitate complex actions performed by the entire body with virtually no deviations. If you feel you are getting good enough to drop this exercise, humble yourself by reading the following stories told by Agnes de Mille:

In the spring of 1948, on the opening day of the Ballet Theatre's season at the Metropolitan Opera House, Nora Kaye, one of the company's two ballerinas, was taken without warning to the hospital with virus pneumonia, three hours before the curtain rose. She had no understudy in *Lilac Garden*. Alicia Alonso had performed it twice six years previously and not at all in the interim. She used the supper hour to refresh her memory under Tudor's coaching, opened the bill with a Balanchine piece, went back upstairs to the rehearsal hall during *Tally-Ho* and then four hours after the first frantic phone call performed the work in question, a role of real intricacy and twenty minutes' duration without a single mistake. Bear in mind there was no score for her to study. This prodigy of memory is in a class with the Toscanini legend; but he has all his needed scores on his library shelves.

A more spectacular example occurred this spring [1951]. In the first movement of William Dollar's *Chopin Concerto*, Norma Vance, first soloist, hurt her foot and was unable to continue. Paula Lloyd, working in the corps, who had merely watched the solo rehearsals, stepped in a few bars later and finished the ballet to the end without rehearsal of any kind. What's more she maintained her place in the ranks simultaneously stepping in and out of the solo role as need arose. It was this extraordinary act of professionalism that prompted Virgil Thompson to remark beside me, "These are the most highly trained people in the theatre, far, far better disciplined than opera singers." [1]

Other activities that will be helpful to you in terms of the development of your coordination include those sports that require skill rather than strength, with particular emphasis on eye-hand coordination. Tennis and Ping-Pong are excellent because it is so easy to arrange to play them whenever one is in the mood Throwing darts or bean bags at a target is of value, as is jumping rope. If you have the opportunity to study fencing, do so.

Some physical activities should be avoided

---

[1] De Mille, Agnes. *Dance to the Piper*. New York: Bantam Books, 1954, pp. 300–301.

because they are of little help in developing your coordination, and in some cases genuinely harmful. They include exercises designed only to develop the skeletal muscles, such as weight-lifting and isometrics. Since as an actor you will have no particular need for great strength, you should never sacrifice the development of coordination to the development of strength.

You should keep in mind also that before you undertake any exercise program which requires much more strenuous activity than you are used to, you should visit your doctor for a physical checkup in order to make certain that your health will not be endangered by such a program.

In this chapter we have discussed exercises that provide a firm foundation for other, more specific exercises. They should benefit you not only in your development as an actor, but also in many other areas of your life. In the following chapters we shall discuss exercises that are specifically designed to provide greater flexibility and subtlety in theatrical performance.

Chapter VI

BUILDING THE BACKGROUND

When you look at a painting you see forms that stand out. You are not as aware of what they stand out from, but if there were nothing for them to stand out from, they would not stand out. The background is an important part of any picture. It is also an important part of movement. Every gesture uses as a background that part of the body that is not drawing attention to itself. The exercises we are going to consider now are designed to help your body build the background that is needed for any gestures it will perform.

First, however, we must understand that you go through three stages as you are learning to use movement as a means of expression. First you will gain increased command of your body by loosening your muscles. Second, as you think about the way your muscles feel, as you find yourself in positions you have never been in before, you will begin to understand movement intellectually. You will create new movements in your mind and attempt to make your body perform them. While you are bobbing in stride position, for instance, you may begin to imagine how it would feel and look to do the same kind of bobbing standing up. Moving in these new ways will further increase your tendency to imagine untried movements. Finally, after much work in the first two stages, you will suddenly find yourself "thinking" with your body. No longer will you have to transfer ideas from your mind to your muscles. Your muscles will

seem to do the thinking. While your voice is expressing an idea in words, your body will express the same idea in movement.

The exercises in this chapter and most of those that follow should be done with a rhythmic or musical accompaniment. The rhythm of the music will help to establish a rhythm in the physical movement.

Stride Position

First, change into loose comfortable clothes. Find a suitable spot on the floor and sit with your legs outstretched and spread as far apart as possible. You are now sitting in stride position. Sit tall: head up, back straight. To relax and hurt at the same time is your first task. You do not want to pull or strain your muscles, but you do want to loosen them. Allow your body weight to pull your head as close to the floor as possible (Figure 8). Some of us are naturally more flexible than others. Do not be surprised, therefore, if your head does not go very far down. The important thing is to make yourself feel heavy, head down, and at the same time to relax the muscles in your legs.

Give yourself three minutes in this position. You will probably notice a gradual loosening; your muscles will seem to separate slightly from the rest of you and your head will drop lower and lower. While the time is passing, think about the way your muscles feel. You will be aware first of the muscles that hurt, but force yourself to think also

Figure 8

Figure 9

about your fingers, your neck, and your feet. When your time is up, grab your ankles and gently pull your torso to the floor. A steady bobbing is the best rhythm to use. This process will loosen muscles you will later want to use.

In the same position, return to an angle of ninety degrees. Touch the lowest part of your back. Now imagine that as you repeat the bobbing process that part of your back is coming through the front of you. Keep your chin out and your head back. Your chest is in the lead. Be aware of your back muscles as your chest nears the floor. You will not go as far down this time. The object is to keep your back straight and your chest in command. When you are practiced at this, your chest will collapse easily on the floor and there will be no curve at all in your back (Figure 9).

During these, and all of the exercises, consciously make yourself aware of your chest, as it is the origin of all convincing movement. How do your feelings change as your chest changes positions? Note your sensations as your chest is first sunken and later stretched and open. Try to relate the action of your chest to the action of your solar plexus (the place where you get the wind knocked out of you). Establish an interplay between them so that the emotions you feel in the pit of your stomach can reach up into your chest and blossom there. (For further clarification of this idea, see Chapter X.)

Long-Sitting

Move now into *long-sitting*. Your legs simply move together until your thighs, knees, and ankles are touching. Your muscles may protest the change. Take it slowly and they will adjust. In this position, repeat the same sequences you followed in stride-sitting. Collapse first, head touching your knees (Figure 10). Move into a slow bob with a rounded back and then into the same rhythm with a straight back (Figure 11).

Notice how much tighter the muscles in your calves and behind your knees are in this position than they were in stride position. Does your back hurt? Notice where. Does your neck hurt also? Memorize this strain. In developing your awareness of the exact location of the strain in muscles you are stretching for the first time, you are learning to recognize the many expressive units that make up your body. You want to become thoroughly familiar with them, and with their exact locations.

We live in a point-oriented world. When we walk, sit, dance, swim, and run, our feet tend to point. We do not use a fully flexed foot for daily activity. The unused muscles in your calves are evidence of this. While your head is near your knees, and your hands are holding your ankles, suddenly flex your feet. The muscles that now hurt are some of the tightest in your body. When the calf muscles have become flexible, you will find yourself more expressive and at ease in such simple movements as walking, stomping, stooping, and turning.

To increase flexibility further, return to the ninety-degree angle and point both feet. Flex them (toes toward the shin). Point them (toes toward the floor). Repeat. Concentrate on reaching your shin. Concentrate on reaching the floor.

Still in long-sitting, sense a pole running from the floor straight up your spine to your head. Throughout the exercise, your back must touch the pole. Lift one leg without bending the knee. Did you knock the pole down by bending your back? Try the other leg. Alternate in a steady rhythm. Some of us in this position can lift a leg no higher than an eighth of an inch. Twenty-four inches is possible for some. The purpose, however, is to feel your thigh muscles at work, and to notice the work your back is doing just to stay upright. When you have lifted each leg eight times, "shake it out." Make a habit of this whenever your muscles feel tight after an exercise.

Figure 10

Figure 11

Frog-Sitting

Take a deep breath. Move, slowly now, into a *frog-sitting* position: knees bent, soles of your feet touching each other, heels as close to your body as possible (Figure 12). Your goal is to get your knees to touch the floor. Press your hands on your knees, pushing them first to the floor, then releasing the pressure. Collapse. Repeat the process sixteen times. In this position try to relax by letting your body weight pull your head down over your legs (Figure 13). Still in frog-sitting, again place your hands on your knees. Keeping your back straight, slowly lower your torso; when you have gone as low as you can without losing your balance, bring yourself up again, keeping your back straight.

Repeat the same bobbing sequence, aiming your chest for your feet with a rounded back (Figure 14) and then to the floor with a straight back (Figure 15). New places will hurt. Pay attention to the new strain. You will feel strain primarily in your knees, your thighs, and your ankles.

Still in frog-sitting, extend both arms above your head. With your chin high, reach with conviction toward some object on the ceiling. Your face will have a tendency to wrinkle and tighten. Relax your face and transfer that intensity to your arms and legs. One at a time extend each arm beyond its natural length. Feel the pulling as it seems to lift your rib cage away from your pelvis. Inside, under the rib cage, in the solar plexus, is where reaching begins. Feel the energy surge from your ribs to your shoulder through your elbow and out your fingertips. Your hands must be alive. When you can convince an observer that you want something on the ceiling, you are truly reaching.

Side-Sitting

With one leg bent in front of your body and the other bent so that the foot is pointing behind you, you are in *side-sitting*. In this position you will experiment with twisting, lifting, falling, eye focusing, and finger energizing. You should learn the physical sensations associated with all those activities.

Twist your torso as far toward the back leg as possible and touch your nose to the floor (Figure 16). Return to a sitting, forward position. This exercise will take you from the upright position to the flattened one in one movement, full of force and energy. To enhance the simple movement you just did, let the "outside" arm, the one corresponding to the front leg, reach into the air and begin moving through space as your torso twists. Bring the trailing arm around in the same manner, keeping every finger alive and both arms completely outstretched (Figure 17). As you twist, lift your face to the ceiling so that your entire torso focuses up, your eyes focusing on the ceiling. Then let your body fall back until your face and arms are on the floor behind you (Figure 18). Your return should be as strong and alive as your fall. Begin with the inside arm first, the outside arm trailing. Untwist until you have reached your original forward position. Do the entire process eight times. Concentrate on reaching (both with the fingers and with the eyes), twisting, and falling.

As you do the exercise, think about the first day you felt your lungs fill with spring air and you ran down a hill, letting your arms and chest fly with the wind. That is the feeling of *up* you should have now. As your head falls back, imagine the sudden control you forced on yourself when you reached the bottom of the hill, as your isolation was broken by people staring at you; you needed to turn away from them, to look down, to hide within yourself; you resented the fleetingness of the moment. But then as you untwist and lift your torso to return to your original position, imagine your ability to recapture the moment in spite of observers. It is all there in the fall and in the return: joy, resentment, determination. Memorize those physical sensations.

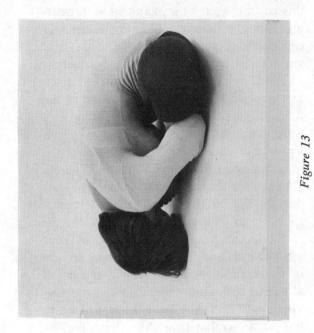

Figure 13

Figure 15

Figure 12

Figure 14

Figure 16

Figure 17

Figure 18

Standing Twist

To further your understanding of twist, stand now and spread your legs in a comfortable stride. Your arms should be out and to the side. You will resemble a weather vane. In a moment you will be turning the upper part of your body above your waist in one direction while your hips will seem to go in the other direction. Your legs and feet remain firm. You will want to focus on the object directly behind you, keeping your arms the same distance apart as you twist. Turn first to one side and then to the other, eight times each.

Although it is primarily the waist that is the center of the twist, notice how many other parts of your body are necessarily a part of it also: your rib cage, your shoulders and arms, your head, your legs and toes. You might associate the twist with the pain of rejection. Try associating another emotion with this action, and see how it brings your body to life.

Feet

As proportionately small as they are, your feet provide the foundation for everything you do. Success or failure in communicating action depends largely on how you use them. Their flexibility and strength can provide you with a world of meaning, lend support to everything you say, and at the crucial moment, take your body into a sudden turn or run. When they seem to move lifelessly, when your inability to do anything with them seems to make them ten times as big as they are, you need to come back to the exercises you will do now and develop your foot muscles.

To strengthen your ankles, stand with your heels together and your toes apart. Slowly rise to "half-toe" (Figure 20). Your tendency will be to put your weight on your little toe. This is a dangerous habit. Too much weight there could cause you to lose your balance and twist an ankle. Instead, consciously put your weight on your big

toe. This does not mean that, like a ballerina, you are standing on your toe. It is still bent, but the weight should be concentrated there. Return to your original, flat position. Repeat this rise and sink many times, until you begin to feel a strain in the lower part of your calf. Shake out your legs.

Do the same sequence again, this time increasing the pace until you are jumping. Once in the air, notice whether your hips protrude and how much noise you make when your feet hit the floor. Try it again; keep your hips pulled under toward the front of your body so that your descent is softened. Puppets are better jumpers than people because a puppet has a string tied to his head that brings his whole body up in a straight posture. Imagine a string tied to your head, pulling you up. Imagine strings tied to your feet and connected to the floor, pulling your feet down to a point. Once in the air you should feel completely extended. As you fall, you will gather yourself into a *plié,* so that your impact is broken.

Plié

Your thighs are weak. Yet they do more to get you through the day than any other part of your body. You sit with them, you walk with them; they take you quickly up and down stairs, they get you to the floor and up again. Wherever you want to be, you must use your thighs to get there. To be of greatest use to you, they must be strong.

Stand in a loose stride. Again imagine that pole down your spine. Gradually bend your knees, keeping your heels on the ground. Return then to your original straight position. Repeat this slow sink, going deeper each time, but not lifting your heels from the floor. Feel the pull in your thighs, in your calves, and in your *straight* back. Figure 19 shows how you will look if your back is straight. If you do the exercise *incorrectly,* you will resemble Figure 21.

After you have done this simple *plié* many times, try it again, looking up with your chin. As you sink, *see* the sky (Figure

Figure 21

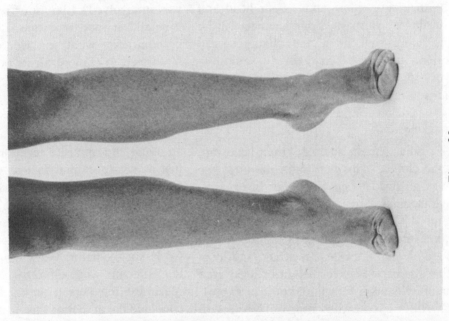

Figure 20

Figure 19

22). What happened to your balance? And where did the pole down your spine go? Try again until you can retain the straight line and keep your feet firmly planted on the ground. Reverse this feeling now by dropping your head and chest and arms between your legs (Figure 23). Your torso is relaxed but completely supported by the strength in your thighs. In doing these exercises, do not allow yourself to stiffen. That will only make them more difficult. Relaxing and controlling your body at the same time is the key to the success of all of these exercises. A variation on the above is to raise your arms as you sink. Let them take their time going above your head and returning as you rise. Your balance will be even more shaken by the change. Keep working until you can do it all smoothly. Every so often shake out your legs or touch your toes a few times to ease the tension.

Neck and Chin

Familiar phrases such as, "their heads are in the clouds," "his nose is in the air," "he hangs his head," "she tosses her head"—all have meanings suggesting character or state of mind. The position of the head is very important in expressing attitude. Being aware of what your head is doing, and loosening the neck to give the entire head area flexibility enough for many kinds of expression, will increase your range of projection substantially. For this exercise, retain your position with heels together, toes apart, legs straight. Isolate your chin and draw a curved line with it through the air until it touches your legs (Figure 24). Take it up your legs and "into" your stomach, then up your chest and back to the beginning. Imagine a pencil on the end of your chin and use it to draw a circle in the air.

Next, in a comfortable standing position, collapse your head—just your head. Do you know that it weighs at least twenty pounds? Concentrate on that weight and let your head roll from down, to the side,

back up, to the other side, down again, and so on. Let the weight exaggerate itself.

Now take each of those areas alone. What does it do to your attitude to hold your chin up? To hold your head down? To hold it back? When would you bend it to the side? What would you be saying in any of those positions? Keep it rolling and find the differences in your attitude. Then stop at the intermediate points between positions. What difference does an inch make in your feeling?

Go back now to the *plié*, using your head as you descend. What do you feel when your head looks up that you didn't feel when it was uninvolved? Like your feet, your head is small but very important. It can reinforce or contradict what you would like to say. You need to explore all its possible expressions.

Reaching

Newton said, "For every action there is an equal and opposite reaction." Actors are just as aware of that fact as physicists are, for every movement they make depends for its effectiveness upon the highly cultivated awareness of action and reaction. Let us explore now the ways in which the concept works for the actor. We will begin by reaching. Imagine yourself onstage. Your arms reach for the person across the room. To convince the audience that your heart is also reaching, you must make your hips and legs pull ever so slightly in the other direction. The stronger the pulling, the more convincing the reaching.

Try this exercise: Stand with both feet facing forward. Lift one arm to the side and look in that direction. See something on the wall and imagine that you want it very much. Reach for it. Your body leans in that direction naturally, but there is a limit to the angle you can create. Too far, and you will fall. So it would seem there is a limit to the intensity with which you can reach. You may feel very strongly about what you are doing

Figure 22

Figure 23

inside, but with only the reaching to express the feeling, your communication is limited.

The solution is to pull with your hips and legs (although your feet will not move) in the other direction. As half of you goes one way, the other half will go just as strongly the other way, and there is no end to the range of feeling. Your focus is on the thing you are reaching toward, so the combination of antithetical movements seems to be all one movement (Figure 25). As an actor, you will probably never take this opposition of forces to its extreme. The dancer may do so, for the farther it goes, the more abstract it becomes. You will want only to understand the extreme so that your muscles will know how much pull is necessary in any reaching situation.

Kneeling

One final set in your daily sequence of movement will take you again through the air. This time your knees will be the base. Kneel first, and then sit back on your heels. Double up, touching your forehead to the ground and finding a place for your arms alongside your legs (Figure 26). This is the opening position.

The object is to lift your torso, hips, and thighs, arch your back, and return (Figure 27). As you lift, your arms should free themselves from your side and move through the air until they have made their own circle and are touching the floor near the sides of your feet. Do not try to extend the circle over your head or to touch the floor behind your feet. That would put unnecessary strain on the small of your back and would accomplish nothing. Instead, concentrate on the way the air feels as your fingers are alive through it. As you lift off your heels and your arms begin to rise, take a deep breath. Exhale as you begin to arch your back and as your arms fall to the side. Your return should be as strong and as alive. It will be more difficult to give strength to the initial lift as you return because you do not have the leverage. But it is possible to do so, and the

feeling you will glean from it is important. Take a deep breath as your arms come up and your back begins to straighten. Exhale as you lower your torso onto your knees. Your back muscles will awaken, your thighs will strengthen, and your head and hands will have created a mood.

The exercise will eventually strengthen your thigh muscles as well as loosen your back, neck, and stomach. To accelerate the growing flexibility of your thighs, however, you will find the following exercise of great help. Begin kneeling. Notice kinesthetically where your back is, and align it accurately with your thighs and buttocks. You should have a straight line running through those places. The exercise involves a simple but steady leaning, with the back of the body approaching the heels. The object is to keep your torso straight as you lean backwards (Figure 28). You will immediately notice thighs. The farther back your torso goes, the greater the support from the thighs. Do not lean so far backward that you cannot pull yourself up into your original position. Leaning back and pulling up several times a day will eventually give you a great deal more thigh control.

SUMMARY

The exercises in this chapter must become a daily experience. Only by increasing the strain will you eventually reduce it. The cruelest thing you can do to a muscle besides allowing it to atrophy all its life is to give it a taste of awareness and then cut it short because you could not find the determination to change your daily routine to include regular exercise. When it hurts, work all the more rigorously. Feel comforted that the strain is your mark of excellence. As time goes on, if you do not learn to love strain, you should at least learn to respect it as an indication of progress.

When you are not actually exercising, think about your body. When you are walking to class, talking on the telephone, beginning to drop off to sleep, what are your

Figure 24

Figure 25

Figure 26

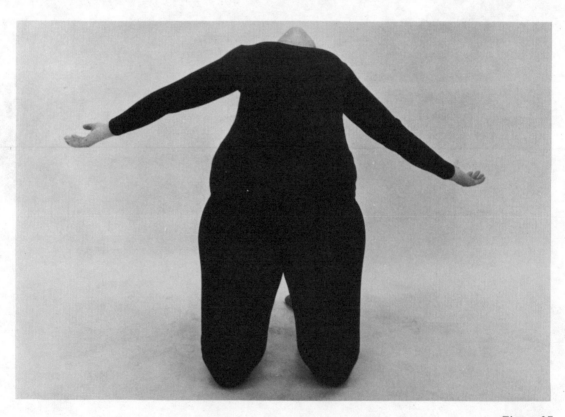

Figure 27

Figure 28

muscles doing? How is your body telling the world about your personality? Notice the changes that take place in your life because you are more aware of and in control of your body. As your awareness increases, your sensory perception in every area will change. You will listen to music kinesthetically as well as intellectually and emotionally; you will react to visual images with the pit of your stomach as well as your mind; and you will gain new confidence in yourself in every situation.

Chapter VII

BREATHING

The most important thing you do is also one of the least obvious—that is, until you are no longer doing it properly. Breathing is the immediate source of energy in movement. Done poorly, it will limit the quality of movement by lowering its efficiency. Done well, it becomes an excellent source of stamina and control.

Breathing is really very simple, and would be much simpler were it not for the fact that in the process of learning to speak we sadly confuse our breathing habits. When you were born, it took you less than a minute to learn to breathe properly. Now that you are older, it may take you years to relearn what you learned so quickly then.

If you want to know how good breathing should look from the outside, watch your dog or cat while he is asleep. Notice that the rise and fall occurs in the lower part of the rib cage, *not* the upper part. Now take a deep breath yourself. Did your chest and shoulders rise up and your stomach go in? You have the process exactly in reverse of the way nature intended you to breathe. You are actually restricting the amount of air you can take into your lungs when you breathe in that way.

To understand why that is so, let us examine a few simple facts about the anatomy of breathing. Your lungs, which are just inside your rib cage, have no capacity to move on their own. Air rushes into them when space is created for it as a result of the expanding of the muscles surrounding the lung area.

Your objective is to move those muscles as far away from the lungs as possible.

The three sets of muscles that should concern you are those that control the action of your rib cage, those that surround your body just below the rib cage, and the diaphragm. The rib cage is so constructed that it increases its capacity most effectively by lifting at the bottom. Bringing your bottom ribs up and in a little will help to expand the upper part of the chest. The diaphragm is a sheet of muscle that runs horizontally through your body at the base of the rib cage, separating the lung area from the viscera that lie below. In the front part of the body it curves somewhat downward. It is by pulling the diaphragm out and down that one most increases the volume inside the lungs. If you can sense where your diaphragm is inside your body, you can actually push it downward. The easiest way to control it, however, is by expanding the muscles beneath your rib cage. Think of your body as a cylinder, and in the area of your stomach increase the circumference of the cylinder.

Now that we understand a little better how the breathing apparatus is constructed, we can see why it does not help to lift the upper part of the chest and the shoulders, restricting the abdominal area. The hiccup-like action of learning to speak has given you bad habits, which you must break. Once you break them, you will not only increase your capacity to take deep breaths and control them, you will also get rid of much of the tension that occurs in the neck area when you are speaking forcefully or breathing heavily as a result of physical activity. This tension affects the organs of speech, decreasing the quality of the sounds they produce.

In normal breathing, only a very small percentage of the total lung area is used. Many people go through life without using much more than that small percentage. When the lungs are not properly exercised, large sections of them may become temporarily unusable. When that happens, it requires several weeks or months of proper exercise rather painfully experienced before the lungs are operating at full capacity, and exercise becomes easy.

When performing a demanding role, you are likely to need much more oxygen than is supplied by normal breathing in order to meet the combination of vocal and physical demands you are making on yourself. If your lungs are out of condition, the performance peaks you can reach will be severely limited, and you will probably never rise above supporting roles that are not too demanding. It is important, therefore, that you increase your lung capacity and control your breathing.

Another reason for learning to control breathing is that whenever an unusual situation arises, the muscular behavior of the body changes, and breathing is affected. The effects of stage fright are very real, and they result from rapid, shallow breathing, which causes coordination of the voice and body to go out of control. When you have learned proper breath control you will no longer have any difficulty dealing with stage fright.

Let us make clear that lung capacity and breath control are two separate things. Improving one does not improve the other. There are three things you can do to increase your lung capacity. The best of them is engaging in regular exercise such as jogging or swimming. If you are getting adequate exercise of the kind that makes you breathe deeply, you will improve your lung capacity. A second kind of exercise is the type of deep-breathing exercise associated with the study of yoga. A third kind of exercise, which you should practice with extreme caution, is simply holding your breath. The more air you can get into your lungs, the longer you can hold your breath, because of the increased amount of oxygen your lungs will have to draw on. You should be wary of this exercise because rapidly taking several deep breaths in a row can flood your brain with oxygen, causing you to lose consciousness.

Increasing your lung capacity increases the amount of energy you have, since the oxygen in your blood makes it possible to burn calories. Since the objective is to get energy to as many cells in your body as possible, you want to enlarge the size of your blood vessels as well as the capacity of your lungs. Therefore types of exercise that involve your whole body should be the most effective.

We turn now to a consideration of breath control. The techniques of breath control can be extremely complex, particularly among those who study singing, and may take years to master. We shall consider here only those techniques that are basic enough to be self-taught. You may find that you do not need to work with all the techniques listed below. Some people are more conscious of the process of breathing than others.

Begin by trying to discover what your body does when it breathes naturally. Lie down and relax as much as possible. Place both hands across your stomach and feel the natural rise and fall there. Press your back against the floor so that you can feel the muscles flattening out against it as you inhale. Sense the difference between inhaling and exhaling. Inhaling is accomplished by tensing certain muscles, exhaling by relaxing them so that they return to their former position. Try to get your entire body so relaxed that no part of it has any tension except the breathing muscles. This will help you to become aware of the action of breathing.

When you have observed the process of breathing in yourself, you are ready to take the first steps toward controlling it. Stand, now, with your hands against your stomach as before. Push out, against your hands, and at the same time inhale. Try to coordinate the two actions. Breath in, hands out (Figure 29). Then reverse the process. Breath out, hands in (Figure 30). You may experience some confusion at first, because you want to let your hands go in as you breathe in. Fight that tendency. At the same time, avoid getting so enthusiastic that you breathe too much too rapidly and cause yourself to faint.

When you are certain of the proper in-out relationship described above and no longer have to think about which way your hands will go in relation to your breath, you are ready to put your hands around your sides so that you can include more of your body in the expanding process. Again, push your hands away from you and then squeeze the air out of you.

Your next step is to begin relating controlled breathing to speech. Count to ten in a whisper, all on one breath, feeling with your hands the gradual and even release of breath so that the entire amount is used by ten. When you whisper, you find it easy to make speech originate from the diaphragm. You probably also find that whispering is much more exhausting than normal speech. That is because you are not accustomed to using so much of your body in the speech process.

Continue counting to ten, each time adding a little bit of voice on top of the whisper. If you lose the whisper when you put in the voice, that is a sign that you find it difficult to make speech originate from the diaphragm. Probably you are tensing the muscles in your throat surrounding the larynx and as a result finding it difficult to make contact with the muscles lower in your body

which should be supporting your speech. If it is extremely difficult for you to combine whisper and voice, you are going to have to relax your whole body completely in order to relax the muscles in your throat enough to let the breathing muscles take over the speech-supporting process. Practice speaking very softly, your whole body relaxed, shifting back and forth between voice and whisper until you are able to combine the two. You will need a great deal of practice in this relaxed position before you can begin to make more strenuous demands on yourself. If you are having this much difficulty it is probably because you have been practicing speech or singing under strenuous conditions and without proper support. You are going to have to unlearn some habits that have become rather deeply ingrained. If your efforts to gain proper support for your tone produce no results after a reasonable period of time, it may be that you have problems with your vocal system that require the help of a speech therapist.

Once the transition has been made and you can easily combine whisper and voice, you are ready to begin controlling the relation between the two. When the amount of whisper is greater than the amount of voicing, the voice sounds breathy. A breathy voice makes inefficient use of breath support, letting out too much breath for the amount of sound that is being made. Closely associated with a breathy voice is likely to be a feeling of breathlessness. Some voices sound breathy even when the breath is properly controlled. This may result from a larynx that has never recovered from early strain. A person who screams excessively may develop nodes on the vocal cords that persist even after he has reformed his behavior. Sometimes they have to be removed by surgery. Inadequate support from the diaphragm combined with excessive strain in the throat are likely to produce such difficulties, too, which is why it is so important to learn to speak with proper support.

You should be able to make the transition

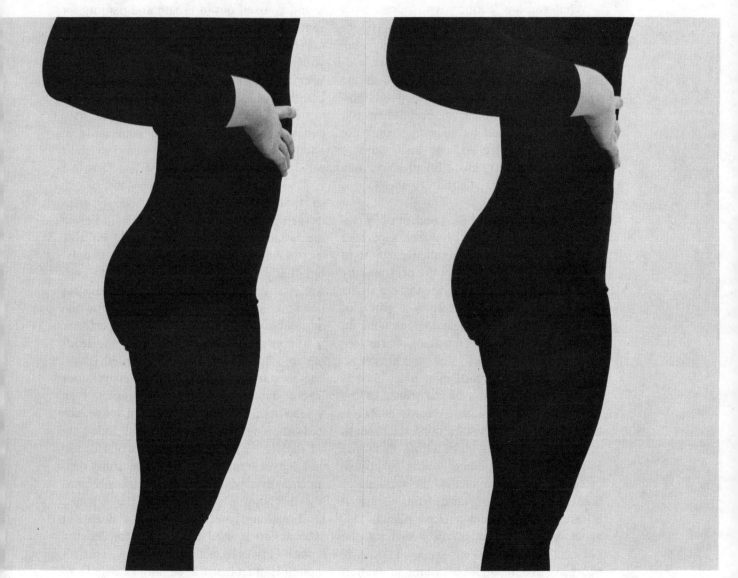

Figure 29   *Figure 30*

from a very breathy tone with a great deal of whisper in it to a bright clear tone that seems to have no breath in it at all and yet is fully supported from the diaphragm. With practice you will be able to alter the ratio of voice to whisper at will and produce a number of interesting and varied vocal qualities.

What you are learning is to release only the amount of breath you need to produce the sound quality you want. You are using your perception of the sound you are producing to make subtle adjustments in the operation of your muscles. Consonants present a special problem in breath control, particularly "f" and "s." These, if they are not properly controlled, can be a kind of escape hatch for too much breath. You may have to pay special attention to them for a while.

Next let us consider the concept of *phrasing*. A phrase is a unit of speech separated by breaths. It is what is called a "thought group," which is any group of words making up what the speaker perceives to be a single thought. In music, a phrase is a group of notes that makes a single logical unit. In singing, the thought groups of words are usually associated with musical phrases, so that one takes a breath in a place that is right for both the words and music at the same time. That is because the composer has built his musical phrases around the thought groups in the words he is setting to music. Phrases vary from single words to groups of sentences. Consequently, the amount of breath that is needed varies from phrase to phrase, and the speaker must plan in advance how much breath he needs for the phrase he is planning to speak. Thus it is necessary to think about breathing in relation to speech, and to associate depth of diaphragm action with length of phrase. When you have learned to "tank up" for a particularly long phrase, you will have learned the kind of deep breathing that is associated with controlled physical action.

We are concerned in this book with physi-cal action rather than speech. Why then so much attention to speech at this point? You will find that breath control is most easily learned in connection with speech, and that what you learn can then be applied to movement. Consider, now, the relation between breathing and strenuous action. The last time you ran to catch a bus you probably found yourself out of breath and panting for some time. That is because you tried to make the shallow breaths that characterize your normal breathing support you in a strenuous situation. You took many shallow breaths instead of a few deep breaths. That not only failed to provide you with the oxygen you needed, it involved your body in additional strenuous action, since your chest was heaving rapidly.

Try running and controlling the breath so that the lungs are filled deeply with oxygen and have a chance to use it all before the breath is exhaled. You should be able to run while breathing slowly and deeply. Gradually you should become able to control your breath so that you plan in advance how much oxygen you will need for the particular action you are about to perform.

Suppose you are going to play the leading role in the last scene of *Hamlet*. It will be necessary for you to perform a strenuous fencing match lasting several minutes, then to leap upon the King, shouting in vengeance and stabbing him violently, and following all that to lie dying in the arms of Horatio and deliver some of the most beautifully restful lines ever written. This is impossible unless the actor playing Hamlet has planned his breathing carefully so that a deep but even action is used throughout the fencing scene. This even action continues, and although Hamlet is still breathing heavily from the exertion for some time after the fencing match, he is able to give the illusion of calm by not breathing rapidly in shallow gasps that break up the rhythms of his speech.

Once you have mastered the basics of breath control, you can continue to develop your skill without specific exercise. It is simply a matter of thinking about breathing whenever you are doing anything strenuous and trying always to keep your breath deep rather than rapid. Under very strenuous conditions, of course, you will need to breathe both deeply and rapidly. But then you will be doing things you could not do at all without adequate breath control.

The word "inspiration" means, literally, a "breathing in." Prosaic and routine as the process of breathing may seem to you now, you will find as you develop your control of the process that it is, indeed, inspiration. Physically, at least, you will become capable of actions that have a richness and control inaccessible to those who do not control their breathing.

Chapter VIII

FALLING

As an actor you communicate within the framework of an environment. The environment is a combination of space and solidity. You must discover relationships between them and begin to structure the framework. Falling provides an excellent means for doing this. Even if you were never to play a scene in which you had to fall down, the ability to fall would prove useful to you, since in falling you *must* structure. The floor is solidity. The space between you and the floor must be properly organized in your mind, or you will get hurt.

Let us begin, then, by analyzing what you must make happen when you fall so that you will not get hurt. You are probably aware that people who are drunk often fall without injury. That is because they are relaxed and do not try to fight the fall. If you are completely relaxed, you can fall quite a distance with little harm. The more you fight the fall, the more susceptible to injury you become. Learning to fall, then, is also a means of learning to trust your own body.

Suppose you were falling a great distance and you saw the ground rushing up at you. It would be a natural impulse to fight it by extending your arms and stiffening them. If you did so, you would concentrate the entire weight of your body in a relatively small area, and the impact would be felt first by your wrists and your elbows, both of which are comparatively weak. Furthermore, stiffening your muscles would make it more diffi-

cult for your bones to respond to the surface they were hitting and increase the likelihood of their being broken.

You want to fall on those parts of your body that will distribute the weight over the widest area, that do not pass the impact on to parts much weaker than they, that are the least rigid, and that are the most padded. These are your thighs, your buttocks, and your shoulders.

Begin getting acquainted with the ground by lowering yourself slowly onto your hip. Gradually continue on your side until you reach your shoulder (Figure 31). You are mapping out the route you will make your body travel with relationship to the floor. Continue going through the process, gradually speeding it up until you feel comfortable and relaxed about falling. If you have difficulty, you may wish to practice first on a mattress and then on a mat or rug before trusting yourself to the bare floor.

Get enough practice with the basic fall so that you are sure of it before you go on to anything else. Too much enthusiasm at this point could result in broken bones and possibly more severe injury. Learn to trust your body to the point that you can relax completely and at the same time control the direction of your fall. You will find such relaxation very useful the next time you fall accidentally, as you will be much more in control of the fall and able to aim your descent so that you do yourself the least possible harm.

Figure 31

While you are practicing, bear in mind that one of the things you are trying to do is protect those parts of your body most easily damaged by falling. Your ankles, knees, elbows, wrists, and head should all be treated with respect. Although you may find you are able to fall directly onto your knees, avoid doing so. Even if you do not hurt yourself, you will look as if you are, and the audience will cease to think about the role you are playing and worry about you the actor.

When you are sure of the basic fall, attempt to vary it, falling gradually more in the direction of your back and, alternatively, more in the direction of your front. You should discover a number of dramatic falls that are possible for you.

Next turn your attention to the motion that precedes and follows the fall. Most important is a rolling motion that can follow the fall, continuing the original force of motion so that the body need not absorb the impact of a sudden stop. You have seen plenty of this sort of thing in cowboy movies: If you are going to fall off a horse, make sure that you roll for a while after your body reaches the ground.

Now turn your attention to what started the fall. Was it a sudden impact that sent you across the room first? Was it a gradual loss of consciousness that caused your hands to hold your head to keep it from spinning? Was it a too-sudden attempt to change direction? Did you trip over something? You will want to practice all those things as preludes to the fall, making each effective in its own right before adding the fall to it.

Next consider the shape your body makes as it reaches the floor. Do certain parts, such as your knees, stiffen up, destroying the grace of the fall and making it appear artificial? If you cannot avoid that kind of action, you can draw attention away from it by the manner in which your hands and head finally come to rest. Experiment with several final positions.

Now explore the use of antagonistic motion of the kind discussed in the section on *Reaching* in Chapter VI. As part of your body moves one way, another part moves in the opposite direction. This can add dramatic flair and interest to your fall. For example, as your hips are moving toward the floor, your torso can be moving in the opposite direction against the fall, so that it occurs in two rapidly sequential stages.

In all of the above exercises and explorations the floor can be a valuable teacher. The floor becomes a measure of how well you have organized space as you moved through it. Every time you miscalculate your action you will get hurt a little. You want to become so expert that you can perform complex and dramatic falls without getting hurt. You will do so by coming to regard the floor as a partner that works with you, not against you, in the accomplishment of your fall. What you learn in this way will help you relate more effectively to the settings, the furniture, and the other actors whenever you are in a play.

Chapter IX

MOVEMENT AS
PERSONALITY EXPRESSION

How is it that you sense another person through movement? Analyze carefully the sensations that you get from watching him, and you will realize that there are complex combinations of tension and relaxation in every personality, which become a key to the understanding of character. Some people seem generally tense, others generally relaxed; but all are tense about different things and relaxed about different things. Imitate another person's movement and you will find that it is necessary to readjust your distribution of tension and relaxation throughout your body.

Let us begin our study of movement as personality expression by examining the extremes. We shall look at tension, examining the emotions that are associated with tightly contracted muscles. We shall also consider relaxation, discovering the ways in which the loose, free body communicates.

First you must study yourself. If your habits of movement include large, lanky strides, a flexible torso, and arms hanging free at your sides, you will want to work particularly hard at achieving the opposite body-feel; you will spend much of your time working with tension exercises. If you are shy and you feel most comfortable with your arms, head, and legs clutched close to your body, you will want to work primarily with relaxation. All of us, regardless of which direction we lean, need to move in every imaginable unfamiliar way.

Having discovered your personal movement habits and preferences, examine the ways those habits reflect your personality by comparing your movement preferences with those of your friends. How would your habits change if your personality changed?

When you feel acquainted with yourself, take some character that you have portrayed or are working on through the same process. Is he an extravert? Is he shy? Try to imagine how his body will express his personality.

Let us try some exercises now to expand your knowledge of body expression. Once again, pay particular attention to the areas least comfortable for you. Your final portrayal of character will probably not utilize any of the movements you will be doing now, but once you have increased your movement vocabulary through these exercises, you will draw upon that reserve to develop specific characterizations.

Relaxation

Relaxing is one of the things people in our culture do least well. It involves a complete giving up—of thoughts, of movement, of worry. In this exercise you will want to experience the extremes of true relaxation and tension. First simply lie with your back on the floor. Relax. Think only of the gradual heaviness of even the smallest parts of your body. Your toes, your fingers, as well as your legs and stomach should all feel heavy and loose.

Now check yourself: When your hand is lifted into the air and then released, it should fall like dead weight to the floor. There should be no tension within it to catch the fall. Have someone lift your hand. If you are either helping or resisting, then you are not relaxed. Try the same tests on your feet, legs, and head.

Tension will give you the opposite feeling and quite a different effect. Tighten your fist; flex your foot; lift an arm and hold it in the air. A second person can test your tension by pressing down on your arm as you press up or lifting your leg while you force it down.

Now, to master the relationships between tension and relaxation in your body, you want to be able to apply each simultaneously in various parts of your body, to shift areas of tension and relaxation quickly, and to do so on command. Have a third person apply tension in one area as the second lifts a lifeless, relaxed part of your body (Figure 32).

Keep the latter loose and use force against the former. Such an experience will help you understand the interplay between the parts of your body and how you can make that interplay more subtle and controlled. As an actor, you will find that one of the chief ways of changing from one characterization to another is to shift the areas of tension and relaxation. The greater the ease with which you can relax and tense the various parts of your body simultaneously, the more easily you will be able to play the most complex characters.

Some of your work will actually combine tension and relaxation in a single movement: A graceful gesture is relaxed tension. In building a graceful gesture, you create tension first, to get the movement under control. You then do the movement often enough so that it becomes more efficient, and less tension is required to control it. Finally, the movement will appear almost entirely relaxed because the amount of tension required

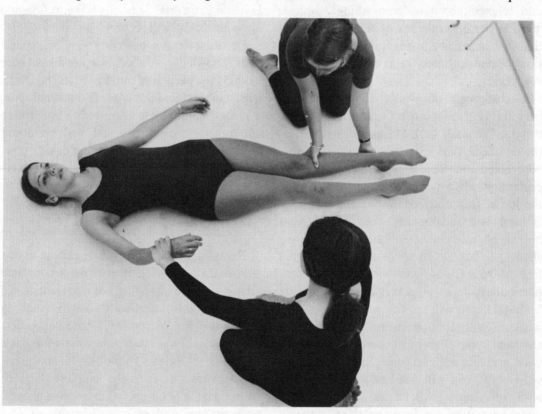

Figure 32

to keep it in place is so slight. It is as if you are coating the original tension with layers of relaxation. Relaxed tension reaches its peak in the work of a ballet dancer sailing through the air. As an actor, you will not develop relaxed tension to so great an extent, but you must always avoid a performance that communicates more tension than would be appropriate for a particular character.

The Importance of Contraction

In. . . . Look at the word. Say it. Let it travel through your mind and try to understand how it makes you feel. Take a short walk around the room, thinking over and over about the concept of *In*. All of us, whether because we are always introverted or because we are momentarily unhappy, live with this concept; and it is its influence that makes us move one way or the other. Think for a moment of your movements during moments of introspection. Do your arms fly out and your legs run happily away with you? Certainly not. You plod along, something in the pit of your stomach grounding you, making you heavy.

If you have recently had the wind knocked out of you, you are at an advantage here. The things your stomach does and the way your chest and shoulders collapse in reaction to being hit are the elements of the contraction which reflect the concept of *In*. Ask a friend to hit you in the stomach, hard enough to make you double up. Notice what happened, how it felt, what your body did in reaction. Try it several times until you can produce the contraction without an external stimulus.

Now, relate that experience to a characterization. Think about the character. He is, for the time being, withdrawn, introverted. You must get to know his stomach. Only there will you begin to know him. Stand in a normal, straight position. Find your stomach with your mind, then with your hand. Isolate it kinesthetically. You are about to contract it. This is a tightening of the mus-

cles much like the effect of the blow in the stomach. The movement of the stomach will resemble the result of the command to "hold it in." But let your shoulders collapse as you do, and let your elbows respond by clutching your ribs. Bend your knees as you contract your stomach, keeping your thighs and ankles touching. Your head should drop, touching your chest with your chin. Stay there for a while. Feel this position with your mind. This is the extreme *In* (Figure 33).

Release

Free your thoughts and your body from contraction and throw them into a gradual but extreme release. Before you move, know that to communicate this change in its extreme, you must straighten your knees slowly while your arms leave your sides. Energy will flow down to your fingertips. Your chest will lift and widen as your head also lifts and you see the sky with your chin. The whole of you is open. Take time to know this release in its entirety, just as you experienced the contraction. Consider the ideas this position can communicate as well as those that cannot be associated with it.

Contract again. Release. Repeat this until you can control every part of your body, until you are saying what you have in mind with every piece of you.

Go back now to lifting just the hand. Realize your feelings as you change dynamics. Quickly, then very slowly: alternate speeds and vary them until you have explored every possibility. How wide is their range of meaning? Try the same with your head. When it is down, how do you feel? When it is up? Vary the dynamics. When you are dizzy, what is your attitude toward your world?

Work next with your shoulders. Contract them. They may go forward toward each other for this exercise; they may go up toward your ears. Release them. Take it slowly this time, very slowly. Then quickly.

Next alternate hands, head, and shoulders, contracting each in turn. Your feeling this

Figure 33

Figure 34

Figure 35

time should be quite different—a little cocky, perhaps. Certainly you will not have the same concern for the total effect.

A more difficult exercise requires the isolation of the chest. You will begin lying on your back on the floor. Open your arms to the side to make a T. The object will be to rise into a sitting position. One's natural impulse is to lift partly from the stomach and partly by pushing with the arm off the floor. This exercise is not a natural impulse. Once again, find your chest. It must be the initiator of the movement. Lift first from the chest, letting your head relax completely as it follows, drooping, after the chest is well on its way up. Your arms are last, fingers trailing (Figure 34). Improve the mechanics of the exercise until you can concentrate on the "open" part of it. Your arms should be behind you, wide open.

The contraction part of the chest lift involves a lifting of the knees toward the chest as it rises from the ground. Again, lie on your back on the floor. With your arms to the side, lift your head and chest simultaneously with your knees and calves (Figure 35). Your chin will hug your neck, and your stomach muscles will contract. Return to the original prone position by stretching slowly, legs, back, arms, and finally your chest. Your head will give up last.

Many times in your own life, in the books you read, and in the plays you will perform, you will find it useful to draw on your knowledge of *contraction* and *release*. Daily exploration of this concept, both physically and intellectually, will build up the reserve that will allow you better to know and portray character.

Having considered the extremes, let us examine more subtle movements. Look at your hand. Make a tight fist, then open your fingers. Carry the action to your forearm. Bring your hand up to your shoulder and down again to your thigh. Combine hand and forearm so that the entire arm is closed, then opened. Try both arms. How do you feel as you do this? Repeat the sequence until, once again, your feeling, not the mechanics, can dominate the movement.

Your daily life is a constant mixture of tension (or contraction) and relaxation (or release). In one way or another you are always using your instinctive understanding of these bodily states. The following improvisation is designed to intensify this understanding and to give you an experience onstage that uses it. The situation involves two people. John is asleep on the floor. Bruce enters, attempting to awaken him. He begins to count, and John responds with numbers. They have until "thirty" to complete the scene. At first John's movement is heavy, very relaxed; he is still not awake, and his reaction to Bruce is negative and slow. Bruce, on the other hand, is quite energetic. There is a great deal of tension in his body and his voice. The object of the sketch is to let Bruce's energy carry over gradually to John, who eventually moves and speaks with as much tension as Bruce had initially. Bruce at the same time is growing tired in his attempt to awaken John. He eventually reacts to John's energy with the same relaxation he saw in John earlier. Ultimately, by a count of thirty, they have exchanged roles.

In any role you may play, you will want to carry the feelings of *contract* and *release* with you. Whether your character is extremely self confident, a case of paranoia, or a struggling mixture, you will need an intellectual and kinesthetic knowledge of these concepts.

Chapter X

THE CENTER OF THE BODY

The most important single concept in any artistic undertaking is the concept of unity. Until many parts have been turned into a single whole that is greater than the sum of its parts, we do not have anything that can be called art. There are many ways of achieving unity in the various art forms. In acting, the achievement of unity is determined by the structure of the body. Everything originates from a single source. What is the center of coordination of all the muscles in the body? When you have discovered it in yourself and have begun to use it consistently, you will find that many movements that had previously seemed difficult will fall into place quite naturally.

Everyone has a sense that "he" is located somewhere in his body. Your arms and legs are your limbs, they are not you. Your head is not you. What is called "you" is somewhere, and if you think about it, you can find it. Probably no two people locate the sense of self physically in the same place. Where you locate yourself is probably more psychological than physical. It does not so much organize your movement as provide an unconscious reference point for your thoughts.

We are going to ask you to locate that physical sense of self and then move it. Concentrate your thoughts on that one part of your body. Make it a center from which all energy seems to flow. Now move that center of energy right into your solar plexus, at the pit of your stomach. If you cannot actually move it, then build a bridge between it and your solar plexus. Get the energy in your body all channeled through the solar plexus.

Next we are going to ask you to plant a seed there in your solar plexus. From the seed a flower will grow. The flower will become your chest. It is struggling to reach outward and upward, toward the sun. But it is always connected by a stem running down the center of your body to the single point in the solar plexus from which it originated (Figure 36).

Now this flower is going to have roots. The roots reach both upward and downward—downward into your legs, and finally right into your toes; upward into your shoulders, and out through your arms to your fingertips.

You might think about that point where you planted the seed in several ways. You might think of it as a light bulb shining up into the flower and down into the roots. You might think of it as a point to which a string is fastened—a string that pulls you toward your objective. Whatever it is, energy concentrates in that point and brings your whole body to life.

Let us go back now to the flower, the blossom, which is reaching for the sun. It will be the liveliest part of you. It will be the chief gatherer of energy, reaching out for it, and sending it down into the solar plexus. You are to make the center of your body a dynamic interrelationship between your solar plexus and your chest, the solar plexus pro-

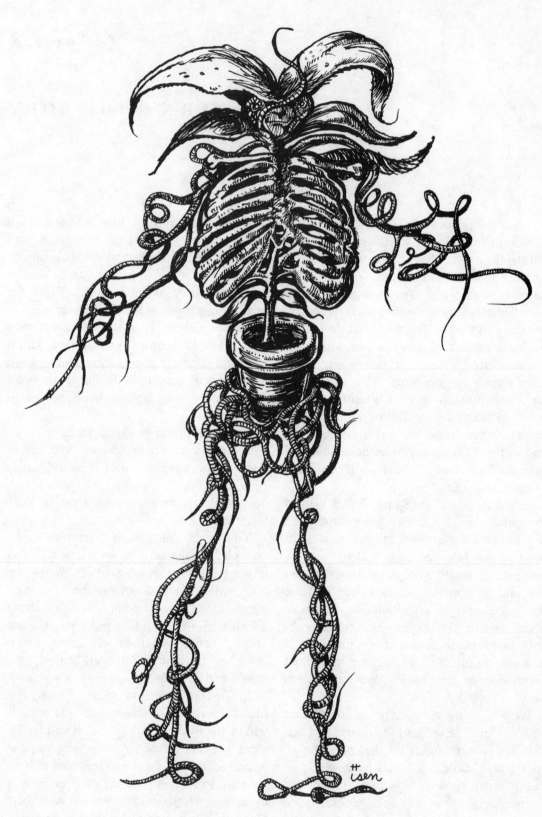

Figure 36

viding the chest with the energy to reach out, the chest gathering energy from the outside and sending it back to the solar plexus. Each enriches the other. Each seeks to make the other feel fully alive.

We shall concentrate for a while on the chest. Find it and notice how it feels. Every time you move you should be aware of what your chest is doing. You will be surprised to discover how much it determines your basic characterization.

Before we examine exercises to improve the use of the chest, think for a moment of the ways in which this center of the body could contradict your words onstage. In a rehearsal, a student served unknowingly as an example of such a contradiction. His line read, ". . . unless we do it ourselves." On that line he was directed to make a strong, 180-degree turn. Each time he did so, he landed off balance, to the side, with his chest collapsed. The effect was, ". . . unless you do it for me." With practice at the exercises we shall discuss here, he was able to say with his body the same thing he was saying in words. A lack of knowledge about the function of the chest had caused the problem.

How does one train the chest? Begin with a contrast of movement similar to the contract and release exercises. As you breathe from your diaphragm, lift your chest. Contrast that feeling with the collapse of air and chest. Walk in this collapsed manner. How would you describe your attitude?

Take another deep breath, and as the air is rushing out, make a continuous sound with your vocal cords. When there is absolutely no more air, begin walking. Keep "pushing" with your voice and be aware of what your chest is doing. You should recall the pain that results when your job is to know the anguish or even the momentary frustration of your character. His feelings will carry across the stage and through the audience only if you are in complete control of your chest.

Next take a sitting position in a chair. Cross your legs. With your hands folded in your lap, collapse your chest. Now lift it. Lift it high until it is too stiff. Tilt it to one side, then the other. Take time to examine the feelings the changes produce. The position of your chest will change your feeling.

Standing with your arms out to the side, isolate your chest. Move it forward without moving your head or arms. Move it to either side and contract it, deep into yourself. Change your feet to an easy stride position, keeping your arms the same. *Plié* several times as deeply as possible, alternating first with a chest collapse, then a chest lift.

Try a walk. Let your chest lead you. It should not lead in such a way as to cause you to lean forward. It should simply be the initial and the continued strength of the walk. Take it into a run. Let it make you feel expanded.

For the next exercise you will need to work on a back road and have a helper. Your job will be to run down the road and convince your helper at the end of it that you are absolutely free. If your chest holds back, even in your mind, or if your head leads instead of your chest, you will appear restricted. Let the breeze you make run with you, not against you.

Thinking "chest" is the key to convincing movement. It is also the key to balance. When our student in rehearsal had learned to focus his thoughts on his chest, his sense of balance was restored. To realize fully the effect the chest can have on balance, stand with your heels together and toes apart. Repeat the half-toe rise you did earlier, but this time concentrate completely on the chest. You will be tempted to think "feet" or "floor" or even "head." But those areas do not control your balance. You will not fall if you are concentrating on the chest as the center of your body.

Carry the same exercise of focus into a jump. Nothing decreases the height of a jump like the collapse of the chest, mentally or physically. Experiment with both. First jump with no concentration on the chest. Then contrast that with a jump that is initiated and sustained by the center of your body. This does not imply a head lift. It is only in the chest.

In your daily life, too, "thinking chest" can be of service. Putting on a sock or shoe when there is no place to sit can be a hazardous experience. Generally more mileage is made by the hopping supporting foot than progress is made in donning the sock. The action can be greatly smoothed and the time spent at it decreased if you simply concentrate on the center of your body. The same is true for reaching to a high place or for squatting to pick up an object from the floor when one arm carries a heavy load. Whenever balance is needed, the center of the body is of utmost importance.

You have thought about your chest. You have used it almost to excess; you have walked in an exaggerated manner; you have jumped high in the air knowing the extra lift the center of your body gives. In your attempt now to put movement together, to make use of these exercises, you will reduce the emphasis on chest movement. Only in the most exaggerated roles will you ever emphasize the chest as you have here. But as with the other movement experiences, you are building up a system of reserves, available to you as needed.

Now that we understand what the chest is to do, we must introduce a note of caution. The emphasized chest must never contort the body, introducing a curvature in the spine. The chest leads from the top, not the bottom, and always has the solar plexus supporting it. The hips are pulled in, backing up the solar plexus, not left sprawling in the background. The chest does not pull away from the body; it leads the body, taking everything else with it. Check your posture in the mirror from time to time, to make sure that the chest is pulling the spine into a straighter position rather than leaving the bottom half of the body behind it.

Let us consider, now, the solar plexus. If you have had the wind knocked out of you, or butterflies in your stomach, you know where your solar plexus is. Your present task is to find it and learn to use it. In the chapter on breathing we discussed the problem of supporting vocal tone from the diaphragm. It will perhaps be easiest to work with the solar plexus if we learn to support the diaphragm (the nearest muscular structure to it) with the solar plexus.

Let us begin with the exercise of piano lifting. Any large heavy weight, such as a desk with three people sitting on it, will do just as well, but pianos are widely available and perfect for the exercise. You are to try to lift the piano in such a manner that the force is exerted with your entire body. You must not strain your back or pull merely with your wrists or shoulders (Figure 37), but rather run the force right down the center of your body so that it is localized in the solar plexus (Figure 38). You start the lift there, and the entire body works together in attempting to lift the piano. Since the force of the weight is equally distributed throughout your body, you are in no danger of straining a muscle. When you have located the force properly in the solar plexus, exert as much pressure there as possible, and count to ten in a loud voice. Under these conditions, the speech must originate from the center of your body, where everything else is originating.

Next, count to ten without actually lifting the piano, but while trying to reproduce in your solar plexus the feeling of piano lifting. Try to keep the same tension in the voice. The tension is there for one purpose only: to help you locate for your present purposes your solar plexus. You are now supporting your diaphragm from your entire body. If you think about it, your arms and legs, even your toes, can be made to contribute to the diaphragm support, for their energy is all channeled through the solar plexus.

We are trying to get the action of the voice and the action of the body to originate from the same source. We begin with tension in order to establish control, and move gradually toward relaxation. The amount of

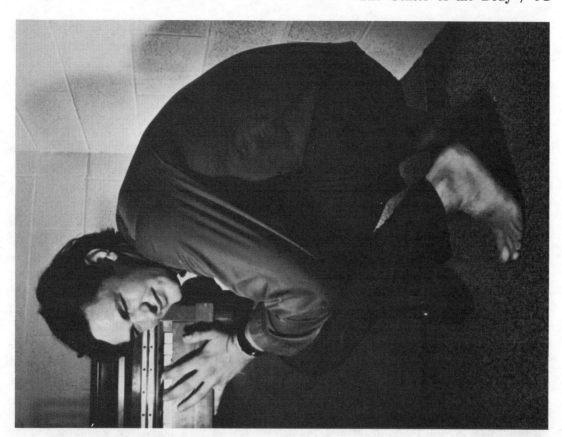

Figure 38

Figure 37

energy needed to establish support in the solar plexus is to be lessened gradually, but as rapidly as possible without losing track of the solar plexus. When you find you can talk from the pit of your stomach, you will be able to "plug in" to the emotions that originate there. You may be surprised at the suddenness with which you can change your voice from a flat and lifeless instrument into one that responds to a wide range of subtle emotions. The effect, once you get it, should be extremely exhilarating.

When you have found the solar plexus as a support for the diaphragm, you are ready to begin to use it for other purposes as well. Remember that you want every action in the entire body to originate there and immediately feed up into the chest as a kind of resonance chamber.

Let us try some sit-ups. Lie flat on the floor, your arms at your sides. You are going to try to sit up, using your stomach muscles only. At first, you will feel the strain near the outer part of your body, in the abdomen. You want to shift the strain to the inside, to the solar plexus, and then distribute it equally from there between your stomach and your back muscles. When you can do sit-ups comfortably with your arms at your side, try them with your arms extended above your head. That moves your center of gravity upward, placing more strain on the stomach muscles. Again, you want to move the strain into the center of your body.

The next exercise involves balancing on the stomach. Lie on the floor face down, arms at your sides, legs together. Arch your back and attempt to roll back and forth on your stomach like a rocking horse. When you can do that with your arms at your sides, try it with them extended above your head, touching your ears. Once again you are trying to move the strain into the center of your body. It will be harder this time, since the stomach muscles are more specifically involved in the rocking motion. Realize that the back is also involved in this action, not just by arching, but also by rocking. Think of your stomach and back as being the two pieces of bread in a ham sandwich. The solar plexus is the ham.

Next we shall work with the muscles of the lower abdomen. Your problem this time will be to shift the strain not only inward, but upward as well. This is much harder, but it is a key to making your entire body share in the strain applied to a specific part of it. You are to lie on your back, feet extended, legs together. Raise your heels eight inches off the floor, separate them, and bring them together again. Try to do this thirty times before the heels return to the floor. Feel the strain in the abdomen and keep trying to shift it to the solar plexus, so that all of your body can help absorb it.

Now let us begin to interpret the meaning of what we have been doing. Stand and place your hand on your stomach. Let your stomach muscles relax so that the entire region protrudes slightly. How does that make the rest of your body feel? Can you feel the drain of energy throughout your body as everything goes limp, unsupported? Even your facial muscles seem to go slightly out of control. Now tighten the stomach muscles and sense the energy flowing back into your body. The more you get a pull from inside rather than a push from outside, the more controlled the action will be. Pay particular attention to the lower abdomen. Is it left lagging behind as the stomach pulls in? Begin the action of pulling in from the lowest part, right in the pubic area, letting that section lead and the rest follow, right up to the ribs. Provide a tight, controlled enclosure of muscles for the solar plexus to work with. Do not neglect the back either. Pull the hips in and under. Straighten the back at the base of the spine. You should get this area so straight that you can lie on the floor with your legs down and have the small of your back touching the floor.

Now walk around, alternating between contracted and released stomach muscles.

Teach yourself the difference in feeling between the two. Memorize what it takes to increase the energy in your body this way.

Let us consider for a moment why it is that you actually increase the energy available to each part of your body by channeling everything through the solar plexus. The idea is actually very simple. Suppose that you tried to lift a piano with your little finger. The muscles in this finger may be strong, but they are not designed to handle a heavy weight by themselves. Support them with the action of your whole hand, and you take much of the strain off them. Still a small part of your body is involved in the task. Back up your hand with your wrist, your wrist with your elbow, your elbow with your shoulder, and your shoulder with your whole body, and step by step you increase the energy available for the task you are trying to perform. As you involve more of your total body in each task, the task becomes easier and less exhausting for any specific part of the body.

When you use your solar plexus to coordinate actions throughout your body, it is as if you called all the various parts of you together to a peace conference. An agreement is worked out whereby there will be reciprocal trade of energies. All the parts agree to supply energy to the part that needs it in time of emergency. Each part will thereby receive energy when it needs it, and provide energy when that part is relatively at rest. Since all parts of your body are burning energy all the time, any energy that is not "lent" in this manner to other parts of the body is simply wasted. When you pool your resources through the solar plexus, you decrease the amount of energy you waste and consequently increase the amount of energy you have. By learning to use your solar plexus you will quite literally discover additional energy in your body and make everything you have to do easier for yourself.

So far we have talked about the solar plexus and the chest more or less in isolation

from each other. As you continue to work with each separately, you should find that gradually they become more related in your mind. You will learn through experience to make them work together. The time will come when you can feel that the solar plexus is the king, ruling over the whole body, and the chest is the prime minister, carrying out the orders of the king and advising him on important matters.

Another thing that will happen as you proceed with the exercises in this chapter will be extraordinarily exciting when it begins to occur. You will someday find that you understand the relation between emotion and physical action. Until that happens, your body will operate somewhat mechanically, going through the motions of exercising without really seeing the point. The transition will occur when you discover that the body is a mirror of the action of the mind. You will feel something, and it will naturally express itself in your body. The realization we are talking about should occur along with your discovery that your body has an inside and an outside.

If you do ten pushups, you can feel the tension in your biceps. These muscles are easy to visualize because they bulge when you tense your arm. They are skeletal muscles that operate relatively near the surface of your body. Most of the exercising you do will tend to make itself felt first in the muscles closest to the surface. Exercising those muscles alone, however, does little to reorganize your body. You may get stronger, but you may also actually impede reorganization. That is why such exercises as isometrics and weight lifting are not particularly good for you. If the body is to be reorganized, it must be from the inside out. It is the positioning of your viscera, particularly your digestive system, that is of greatest importance in how you look and how you move. Exercises that reach in toward the center of your body will help to reorganize you by positioning, lifting, tightening, and bringing under control all the functions of your body. The excitement occurs when you discover those inside sensations and associate them with your exercise. Why?

Listen to music or fall in love and where are you affected? Is it in the skeletal muscles, such as your biceps? No, it is deep inside you. It is in what you may come to visualize as the inner layer of your body that you will localize your emotions. Reaching that inner layer through exercise makes it possible to control what until that point has been involuntary. The time will come when you can pull the strings inside yourself and actually simulate various emotions. You will be able to produce butterflies in your stomach at will. You will be able to simulate the sensations of falling in love, or of grief. You will be able to switch from one emotion to another on command.

To a certain extent you can probably do this already. The point is that controlling the inner layer of your body through exercise will enormously increase the efficiency with which you do it, no matter how good you are now. You will decrease the amount of effort it takes to find a character's emotional condition. You will find it much easier to enter into that state of emotional identification with the character that is usually associated with the Stanislavsky method of acting. You will, in short, have taken your most far-reaching single step toward total artistic control.

Chapter XI

EXPLORING THE EXTREMITIES

The basis of all communication lies deep in the center of the body. Its details are in the extremities. Facial muscles, fingers, and toes will fill in the outlines broadly sketched by the torso, the arms, and the legs. You have yet to discover the incredible plasticity of your body that lies in its infinite resources of detail.

Our first exercise is in the form of a competition. We want to find out in how many positions it is possible to hold any given part of the body. Get together about ten people and compete to see who can hold the shoulders in the greatest number of positions. In order to restrict other forms of body movement, you may wish to use the balance board described in Chapter V.

You are to stand on the balance board and try to hold your shoulders in as many positions as possible. You must be able to maintain each position for at least ten seconds without tipping the balance board. You must not reuse any position you used previously. All that is required is to change the relationship of the shoulders to the rest of the body.

It is probable that the first four or five people who try this exercise will find that fewer than ten positions occur to them. It is equally probable that the tenth person in the sequence will be able to go as high as two hundred. The number of positions in which you can hold your shoulders with relation to the rest of your body is virtually infinite, but you have probably never even

thought of more than a few of them. All that is necessary is to explore in the company of others, and you will begin to discover the richness of movement that is possible for you. You will begin to develop a creative attitude toward the movement of your body.

In subsequent exploration sessions, try working with the head, the arms, the legs, and the feet. Keep working together with your group until each person feels confident that he could continue to assume various positions forever. One of your main limitations as an actor has been that you have not even tried to imagine interesting things to do with your body because it has not occurred to you that much was possible. Once possibilities have been opened up, you can continue to explore the physical details of each character you play. You will learn that a quarter of an inch properly placed can age a character fifty years; that less than that distance is required to turn joy into sorrow. You will learn to avoid the clichés of movement that are so often seen among amateurs and to make every part of your contribution to the stage picture an interesting new development in the physical unfolding of character.

When you have become aware of the infinite variety of possible arrangements of the larger sections of the body, you are ready to be concerned with the fine details. You will feel more comfortable working alone on these exercises.

Become acquainted with your face and

Figure 39

what it can do (Figure 39). Work with a mirror. There are those who argue against this approach on the grounds that it encourages superficiality. What happens in the face, so it is said, must be a reflection of what happens deep inside the emotions. It must not be artificially produced. So far, we agree. If you are going to use the mirror to build up a repertoire of absurd expressions that bear no relation to actual human feeling, you will only make a fool of yourself. Study the emotive powers of your face as you would study its outlines in preparing to apply makeup. You must know what you have to work with and what it will do. All the emotions in the world will not do you a bit of good if they are forever locked inside of you. You must make of your face the book in which an audience may read your emotions.

Look first at what your eyes will do. Without moving any of the muscles except those within your pupils and perhaps the upper and lower lids you should be able to register a variety of emotions. Go from a lazy glance to a penetrating gaze. Change a look of adoration into one of hatred. Can you register twenty-five distinctly separate attitudes with your eyes alone?

Now try the cheeks. What will they do besides smile? Can you make them appear sunken in order to suggest age? Can you tense the area above them, suggesting uncontrollable rage? Move them toward and away from your nose.

You should pay particular attention to your lips. Most people have lazy lips because the habits of everyday speech are not sufficient to exercise them to full capacity. Begin by stretching your lips all the way back to your ears, saying "ee." Then push them as far out as they will go, saying "oo." Alternate until they are tired, constantly trying to push them a little farther.

Now sensitize the inside of your lips. Place your index finger inside them and suck on it. Feel the inner lip as distinct from the outer lip. Use that inner lip when you speak, giving your words a sensuous, liquid quality. Use it to make the lips more supple. Move your lips about at random, exploring the distinction between inner and outer lip. Distinguish between the lips. If the lower lip is held stiff and only the upper one moves, you can learn to speak very rapidly.

How much do your lips move independently of your jaw? Some people overuse their jaws in speech. Put your hand on your lower jaw to hold it in place, and practice speaking, using only the lips to form the words. Now move only the jaw, keeping the lips tight. Alternate between the two extremes until you have a clearer idea of how jaw and lips interrelate in movement.

Eyebrows, mouth, chin, and nose should all be explored in a similar manner. The explorations are merely for the sake of opening up new territory. Your ultimate concern is making all the parts of your face work together to establish a single mood. Obviously, your repertoire of possible facial expressions will increase if you develop the feeling that the opportunities are infinite. Many actors, some of them well known, seem to get by on only four or five facial expressions. There are even those who try to make do with only one—a completely pointless economy that can be avoided with even a minimum of effort.

Beware of "mugging." Actors who consistently use exaggerated facial expressions quickly become annoying to watch. You should be able to exaggerate when necessary, but in general you should cultivate understatement. If the expression is in excess of the emotion that has been established by other means, the effect is ridiculous.

Obviously the same kind of facial technique will not work on the stage as in the films. When the audience is at a distance, a certain amount of exaggeration is essential. You must project the expressions on your face just as you project your voice. In the end, feeling and experience must be your guides in choosing appropriate facial expressions. You will have to do a lot of experimenting before you get the results you want.

Let us now pay some attention to the action of the fingers. They play a very important role in determining the degree of grace that a character communicates. We shall begin by considering the ideal position of the fingers in relation to one another, as laid down for our guidance by classical and Renaissance sculptors. Look, for example, at the extended arm of the Virgin in Michelangelo's *Pietà* (Figure 40). The index finger is extended the most, pointing, but slightly curved. The other fingers are increasingly curved in toward the palm. The middle

and ring fingers form something of a unit, being a little closer together than the others. The thumb points in the same direction as the index finger.

It would be a good idea for you to train your fingers so that they fall naturally into this position when you are not trying to achieve some other effect. Fingers can easily look grotesque, which can be disconcerting during a love scene.

Flexibility of finger movement is associated with flexibility in the wrists. An exercise to limber up the wrists is the following: Hold

Figure 40

your arms so that they extend out from your body, parallel to each other and to the floor. Make certain that the elbows remain stationary. Let the hands hang down from the wrists. With the tips of your fingers, trace a figure 8 in some imaginary sand. In doing this exercise you should feel a pull on one of the muscles in your forearm that you make very little use of. Occasional use of this exercise should bring sparkle and excitement into the actions of your fingers, which should no longer be felt to be an extension of the hand, but should take on a life of their own.

Finally, let us consider the toes. Although they almost never show, since you wear shoes most of the time, they significantly affect what you do with the rest of your body.

The way you come down on your feet affects the way you carry the weight of your whole body. Some people tend to walk on their heels and sink down into themselves, presenting a slightly caved-in appearance. Others walk more on their toes and appear to be leaning forward, peering out at the world. Before going on, reread the remarks on walking in Chapter V.

You can affect a characterization significantly by changing the way you land on your feet. Probably you make little use of your toes. Actively involving your toes in walking, making them feel something like fingers, will tend to bring your whole personality forward a little. If you are playing a very outgoing person, concentrate on communicating with the tips of your lips (using exaggeratedly good diction), with the action of your fingers, and with the tendency of your toes to reach out and become involved in walking. Think of all of these as one action.

An exercise to help you become more conscious of your toes is to use the pointed toe associated with dancing the minuet. With each step before you put your whole foot on the floor, point the toe and just touch it to the floor. Then let the foot come down. This will turn your walk into a kind of strutting that will tend to straighten your back and bring your weight forward. Walking in this manner will help you sense what is needed in the physical projection of any role. It is essential preparation for the portrayal of a role in Restoration drama.

If you are having trouble with the above exercise, it may be that you do not yet have sufficient control over your sense of balance. In that case, return to the section on balance in Chapter V.

We have considered some of the parts of the body that are most subtle in their expressiveness. It is in your work with them that you will perhaps do the most in developing your personal style, as it is in details of movement, particularly of the face and the hands, that actors tend to identify themselves. Perhaps you will observe and imitate some favorite actor in the initial development of your style. This is not to be discouraged, as it is one way to help yourself learn what mature acting is like. It is, however, no substitute for your own style, as the actor you are imitating will always seem better than you do when you imitate him. Imitate, then, as a step in the learning process, but do not expect your imitation to be accepted as a final product. Perhaps you will go through stages of imitating several actors and eventually synthesize the good qualities of the various styles in order to develop your own.

When you are developing your sense of how to use your extremities, remind yourself from time to time that the body must operate as a unit, and that all we have said in the previous chapters must continue to be practiced in relation to what you are doing now. In thinking thus, you will eventually carry yourself beyond exercise to the point that all exercises become one because they all interrelate in your mind through a well-unified body.

PART III—STORY-TELLING THROUGH MOVEMENT

Chapter XII

MOVEMENT AS A
SIMPLE STATEMENT

An actor must come out of himself. Even those whose roles are always of the same nature, whose acting is primarily an extension of their personalities, must explore attitudes uncommon to their offstage lives. Now you must also do so. It is particularly essential if your talents lie in character acting.

In our discussion of contract and release we talked about the necessity of emphasizing exercises least comfortable for us. Let us explore that concept further now. We are going to experiment with movements specifically for the purpose of communicating attitudes. As you do these exercises, your attention should be on what you are saying to an audience with your body.

Try the following changes in position. First bend your knees only half way. Lean the torso slightly forward and put your hands on your thighs, fingers pointing out. You will look like an umpire or an outfielder, and you should remain in this position until you feel assertive and a little sloppy. The picture would be complete with chewing tobacco in your mouth. Vary the position by turning your fingers in, and notice the change of character that results.

Drop into a deep squat and place your forearms on your thighs; let your hands dangle between your legs. Bounce a little, moving your hips off your haunches and back again. Get into the feel of a squat. If you are a young man or a tomboy, you may

feel at home here. If you are a young lady, you will not. This squat exercise is designed especially for young ladies.

You will want to assume many other simple positions in which you should discover a change of attitude. Put your hand on your cheek. You are communicating surprise or despair, or perhaps you are warming your cheek (Figure 44). Put your hands on your hips. If you are not a cheerleader, you are telling your audience that you are strong, confident, and masculine (Figure 45). This is basically an athletic stance and would not be used to communicate anguish or insecurity. Stand tall this way until you feel strong. A slight change, moving your hands to your waist, changes your message from strength to resistance (Figure 46). Try this change. It can be a resting position as well. Still, it is secure.

The most popular position is with arms folded; all of us feel comfortable in some variation of arms folded in front of us. The most common position is each hand under the opposite arm, both arms against the stomach. This can be used in casual situations, although it is fairly inexpressive (Figure 41). A less common variation involves taking the hand that is under the opposite arm and letting it clutch the area above the elbow (Figure 42). Both arms move slightly away from the stomach. This is a stiffer look and is used extensively in

Figure 41   *Figure 42*   *Figure 43*

charm schools to give an air of sophistication.

"Hands typical" for girls in operetta choruses, a stance that is elegant, ladylike, and restful, is to clasp the hands in the center of the body so that the right hand is palm up and the left wrist is elevated slightly (Figure 43).

Unclasp your hands and clasp them behind your back. Men are sometimes taught to take this stance to appear suave and cordial. Then they wonder why their guests are ill at ease and distant. The fact is that there is nothing dignified or cordial about a man with his hands behind his back. It suggests insecurity and subservience. If your role is that of a *maître d'hôtel* or of a wobbling unsophisticate, you will want to use this position. Try it now.

The same kind of insecurity can be conveyed by standing with your legs crossed, feet flat on the floor. Those who do not know what to do with themselves sometimes find their legs entwining. See how you feel in this position. Then at your next social gathering, notice those who flirt with this position—usually for lack of opportunity to flirt with anything else. Notice, too, other kinds of leg and foot contortions. Insecure people find it difficult to distribute their weight equally, and therefore often stand on the edge of one foot, or with one leg out at an angle. Get out of the mess and stand with both feet pointed straight ahead and both knees straight. Now bend one knee; rest on your hip. Sense the new relaxation. Notice the many variations of this position depending on where you place your foot, how much you bend your knee, and where you center your weight. Try several variations in front of a mirror and try to find one that looks particularly dignified.

Let us work with arms and hands for a moment. Put one hand on the back of your neck and the other on your hip. You should feel like pondering the problems of the world. Move your hands in front of your stomach and let your fingertips touch. You

are still deep in thought. Move the hands so that one is clutching the wrist of the other, the latter hand pointing down, both arms fully extended down. Or hold your hands, fingers woven together, in front of your body. You have decided to converse.

From a movement point of view, your arm is divided into three sections. This allows for an extended arm, one bent at the elbow, and one in which the hand does all the work while the rest of the arm is close to the body. Experiment with these sections and memorize the various attitudes and kinesthetic feelings.

In a moment of tension, an arm held close to the body with just the hand loose can communicate far better than an extended arm. To expand your understanding of the arm sections, find seven distinct movements your arm could make with each section. Define the feelings for yourself. Keep the knowledge alive so that at any moment you could call upon it to aid in your projection of a total character.

Now we are ready to experiment with locomotion. Find a helper again and return to the road. You have already shown him the movement of the free run. At that time there was no panic in your body; your head was tossed back; your arms were out, and your fingers felt every particle of air. You were happy as you ran (Figure 47).

Had you been afraid or worried instead of joyous, your helper would have seen quite a different picture. Your arms would have been bent at your side, your feet would have increased their pace quickly. Your head, no longer tossed back, would have been stiff, turning now and then to see the thing from which you were running (Figure 48).

Had your intention been to acquire something of great value at the end of your run, you would have traveled in yet another way. Arms extended forward, full of energy, you would have raced ahead eagerly, impatiently. Your shoulders, too, would have moved, each one going forward alternately to extend your reach. Your head would have faced

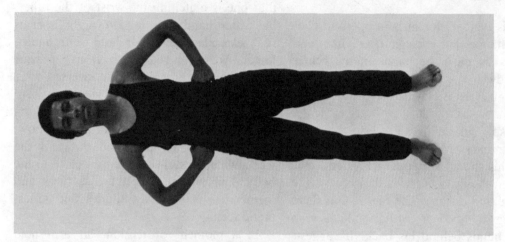

Figure 46

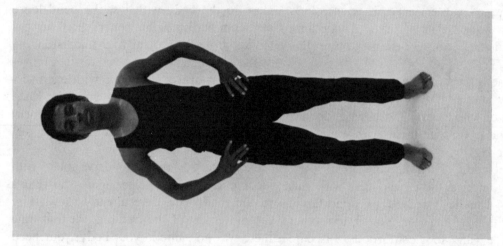

Figure 45

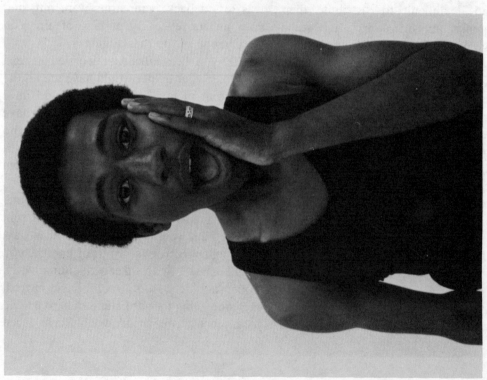

Figure 44

forward, and your eyes would have focused strongly, intensely, on the desired object. Your torso would have bent slightly, completing the picture of full body participation (Figure 49).

Suppose you had been confused. The run would again have been unlike any of the others. You would not have run in a straight line. Your body and your focus would have shifted, first to the right, then ahead, then back and to the left, fluctuating constantly.

There is no such thing as just running. Whatever your motive, your run will reveal it. If your motive onstage is one thing, but your run reveals another, you will confuse your audience.

Try the variations again. After you have run with conviction, communicating each feeling we discussed, combine one movement with another motive. You will find that if your arms fly open and your head falls back, you will not be able to convince your helper that you are afraid. Discover also the various things that *can* be said with the combination of opposing movements. What *are* you saying with fear in your heart and joy in your movement?

Walking

A student cast in a confident, alluring role was distressed because she had one walk across the stage which seemed endless to her. She was directed to communicate all the self-confidence she could while still projecting attention to the character sitting across the stage. Her walk had to get her to the other side of the stage and at the same time say, "I am attractive and I know it. I believe in myself and I am interested in you." No lines were to be spoken here, and without that crutch she lost her characterization. She became young and insecure. She could only consider how far, how dreadfully far, it was from her position to the other side of the stage.

To solve her problem, she explored the full range of walking. She realized first that walking does not involve the legs only. Put yourself in her position now and walk naturally across the room. Imagine yourself walking down the street in no particular fashion. Repeat the natural walk and be aware of your arms, your head, and particularly your chest and shoulders. You may be stooped or slightly swaybacked without knowing it. Return to the discussion of walking in Chapter V and determine in what respects your walk is distorted.

Now, standing in front of a mirror, watch your profile. Change the position of your neck, back, shoulders and head until you see a straight back in the mirror (Figure 5). Tuck in your buttocks and hold in your stomach. When your profile line is straight, you are ready to begin. If it is not comfortable, and you find it difficult to feel at home in this position, walk around in it for a while (for a month or two if necessary). It is from this neutral, straight position that you must begin. Until you are there, you cannot be certain your variations of posture and walk will say what you think they are saying.

Shoulders

The shoulders, like the chest, are essential for a successful walk. From the neutral position, pull the shoulders in toward each other; now pull them back as far as they will go. Lift them again; relax them; and finally move one in and the other back, alternating several times. Work at this movement—one shoulder in, the other out—until it is easy for you. Now combine it with a walk. Slow it down and modify it until you begin to feel proud and seductive. Our student who was worried about her walk across stage used a very modified shoulder alternation as she walked and communicated a great deal more self-confidence than before.

Feet

However, it was more than just her shoulders that changed. Her feet moved differently also. To find just the right step, she first explored all of the possible foot variations. She

Figure 49

Figure 48

Figure 47

repeated her normal walk, this time being particularly alert to what her feet were doing. She then went into a "high walk" on tiptoe, looking up. From there she dropped radically into a "low walk," bending her knees as deeply as she could without impeding the walk, head down, arms in. These were the extremes.

To find the foot action best suited to her role, she experimented with stages between the extremes. Her attitude changed from one variation to another until she *felt* confident in her feet. The chosen walk was relatively high, but not high enough to make her feel haughty.

Try her experiment. Move from "high walking" into "low walking." Move then through all the intermediate stages and notice your feelings. You will discover for yourself what she did with her feet.

Dynamics

Before she was ready to go back to rehearsal, she explored even further. Her walk lacked the right dynamics. That is, she had not yet determined how much energy should be released in her walk. First she responded to the suggestion, "Convince me there are eggs on the floor." Her walk was slow, and very careful, toe first.

Next she walked as if a baby were asleep in the room. This took her into a quiet tiptoe.

She then convinced her director that she was walking through mud. Her movement was heavy and still slow.

Finally, her job was to communicate the presence of hundreds of tiny bugs on the floor. She moved quickly in tiny stomps, a heavy but quick walk, heel first.

She discovered that her alluring walk would be fairly light, but deliberate and fast. It would not rush her, but it would steer completely away from the quiet walk suggesting eggs on the floor.

At last her problem was solved. Her character was convincing, and the stage no longer seemed infinite. She had realized that her

entire body could talk even when there was no dialogue. She no longer feared the silence of her walk; it spoke loudly and appropriately. Words would, for that particular moment, have been superfluous.

Let us suppose now that she had been playing an old woman. To communicate the weariness of the aged she would have used short spasmodic steps, the feet hugging the floor. Her torso would have been stooped, her head drooping wearily from her shoulders.

How different the result would have been had her character been haughty. Her walk would then have been higher, her shoulders back slightly, alternating very slowly.

Had she merely been musing, her shoulders would have moved very little; the emphasis would have been on her head as it moved from side to side or up and down, slowly and sporadically. Her walk would have been slow and aimless, not heavy, but not particularly light.

If she had been tired? Try this. Your head feels heavy and drags under the pressure. Your walk is heavy also, but unlike your trip through the mud, your steps are short and without conviction. If you were at the point of complete exhaustion, your toes would drag; your shoulders and chest would be collapsed. You would communicate under great strain.

Had she been desperate, her walk would have taken on yet another character. The pace would have quickened, the shoulders first in one position, then another. Her head would have moved as, in the run of confusion, her focus changed. Her face might have been in her hands at one point, and a split second later flying in the air while her hands nervously gripped her legs.

Her character was self-assured. What would the difference in the walk have been had she instead been insecure? As we discovered in our exploration of contract and release, a lack of confidence can be betrayed in a number of ways. Overly large steps or extremely small steps are two certain clues.

Take seven giant strides across the floor; then return, using tiny steps. Examine your feeling. Now walk in a stride of medium width. Ask a friend to interpret your walk. Practice will help you reach the point of successfully communicating with your body the ideas and attitudes in your mind.

We have discussed isolation of parts of the body and the innumerable ways single parts can move and communicate. We have also seen how the messages of motor movement are changed by varying the positions of various parts of the body. Let us turn now to more complex actions. In the next chapter we shall take various movements and combine them in order to tell a complete story.

Chapter XIII

MOVEMENT THAT TELLS
A COMPLETE STORY

You are walking down the street and you see an old friend. You greet him effusively. Instead of returning your greeting, he looks past you, raises his nose in the air, and walks on. No words. No need for words. A story has been told about feeling, using only a simple gesture. It would take a good many words to equal the effect.

Having experienced such wordless communication many times in your daily life, you see the dramatic power of it. Now you must use your imagination to develop such moments of dramatic power within the context of the play you are rehearsing. Where can you add to the text with a simple but memorable movement that needs no words? Often playwrights climax their plays with such gestures. You as an actor can enormously enrich the audience's experience by adding others that are in keeping with the playwright's message. Unforgettable theatrical images that set a standard for you include Lady Macbeth washing her hands, Hedda Gabler burning her lover's manuscript, and Liliom slapping his daughter's face. The images you invent may not be as central to the drama as those examples, but they can nevertheless have a profound emotional effect.

Your problem as an actor is to imagine the words that a character thinks but does not speak and then to find movements to represent those words. You will be using movement as another kind of language. You must learn some of the rules of that language so that what you do will be clear to your audience.

Let us first examine the concept of *beginning* and *ending*. Most amateur actors when they gesture put in only the middle of the gesture. It starts indefinitely and disintegrates at the end. Each movement should have a clear beginning and ending, so that we know exactly what its structure is intended to be. Begin with a pantomime exercise. You are closing a bureau drawer. The drawer is at about your chest level, and you are going to use both hands to close it. You will do so to a count of four. The movement is even for counts two and three, but on the count of one the hands snap into position, and on the count of four they come to a definite and sudden halt. You will want to do this a number of times, exaggerating the effect so that the hands seem to snap into place on the beginning and ending of the movement.

Try other simple gestures to a count of four, making sure that the gesture begins abruptly on "one" and terminates abruptly on "four." Try movements using your whole body in this manner. You want everything you do to be purposeful and communicative. Nothing is there accidentally. Nothing simply dies in the air.

After you have experimented with this

111

concept in its exaggerated form for a while, try more subtle gestures that do not begin and end so precisely and obviously, but nevertheless must originate somewhere and not be left hanging. You will discover that you are going to have to think in terms of a series of actions which meld into one another. Your body is always doing something definite, intentional. Nothing is left to chance.

Next let us examine the concept of the *reality* of gesture. All movement relates to emotions, ideas, things, or people. The more abstract movements, that is, those that relate to emotions and ideas, have a reality that can originate only inside the actor. One either does or does not recognize that a particular gesture has communicated an emotion. In order to establish such an emotion, an actor must think through and feel through his character, using the ideas about movement established in previous chapters.

Movements which have a concrete relationship to things and people will be responsible for what the audience perceives. You would not shake the hand of a timid child the same way you would shake that of a professional football player. You need to relate the gesture to the particular qualities of the individual you are dealing with. By the same token, you do not handle a feather and a bag of flour in the same way.

You will improve your understanding of how to move in relation to people and things most rapidly if you study pantomime. As an exercise, stand before a group and handle an imaginary object. The group must be able to guess *from the way you handle the object* what the object is. After you have successfully communicated two or three dozen objects in this manner, start dealing with imaginary people. Again, your audience must guess the characteristics of the person you are pretending to deal with.

One of the greatest difficulties in doing this exercise will be a problem of spatial relations. If you are talking on an imaginary telephone, the position of the telephone will probably change between the beginning and ending of the conversation. It may even change while you are dialing the number. If the objects you are handling do not sit still in space, the effect is disconcerting to watch. The problem stems from the way your orientation changes as your body moves. An exercise that emphasizes the need for consistent orientation is to open an imaginary door with one hand, walk through it, and close it after you with the other hand. Almost invariably the door handle will move several inches. Keep trying it until your audience is satisfied that you have kept the handle of the open door in one place.

In dealing with imaginary people, the greatest difficulty is with height. Time and again the actor will make the height of his imagined partner vary by several feet: sometimes he is way up in the air, sometimes he is lying on the floor. Have your audience stop you every time you vary the height of the person you are pretending to talk to.

You will help your audience visualize whatever you wish them to see by doing something you do not do when dealing with real objects. Use gestures to indicate the general shape of the object. You must do this in such a way that you do not make it obvious that that is all you are doing. If you are handling a box, for example, feel its sides first while considering whether or not you wish to lift it. Then shift and pick it up by holding the top and bottom of it. You will be more successful in pantomime of this sort if you create a character who is carefully exploring his environment as if he expected it to trick him at any moment.

Exercises with pantomime will help you to think more carefully about how to relate effectively to the actual objects you must deal with in a play. In addition, they will prepare you for those actions that occur in many plays that are genuine pantomime. Most important, pantomime will train you to think about what you have to do to make the audience see whatever you wish them to see. As an actor you must always know exactly what your audience is seeing. To the extent that you do not know, you have lost control over your performance.

So far we have talked about movement in this chapter as if it involved only the parts of the body actually performing the movement. In earlier chapters we have established the extent to which all parts of the body work together as a unit. We now wish to call attention to the enormous importance of acting with your eyes all the time you are acting with your body. Your eyes must be as actively involved in every gesture, every movement, as are your hands or legs. That does not mean you have to look at your hands all the time. Your eyes may be focused where your hands are pointing, or you may be looking away from the thing you are pointing to. Whatever the situation, however, the movement will appear lifeless no matter how well it is performed unless the eyes are as much involved in the act as the body. In addition, much of your self-consciousness about gesture will disappear almost automatically once you learn to breathe fire into the action by using your eyes.

Let us now experiment with some storytelling actions that are limited to a single character.

Bubble Gum

First, stand with your hands in front of your chest, fingers and palms touching. Now imagine that between your hands you have five pieces of chewed bubble gum. Move your hands apart with the sticky gum constantly in mind (Figure 50). Continue to move them until you feel that the gum could separate in strands from itself. Make the moment of separation obvious, and do not depend upon your face alone to communicate the stickiness or the relief of the separation.

Let one hand fall on your thigh and the other on your head. Work with this problem until both hands free themselves. Repeat the situation with two other parts of your body. Continue until you have succeeded in bubble-gumming your entire body. One part

sticks to another and to another and hopelessly to another.

Little Thing in Hand

Imagine that you have a tiny sparrow in the palm of your hand. Move the other hand to caress it. Convince your audience that you love it. Transfer it to the other hand in a loving manner. Now in your mind turn this sparrow into a person you love and feel protective toward it. Show your audience with your cheek that you love it. Now move it, still in your hand, and show them the same thing with your thigh (Figure 51).

The movement is slow and tender. Your eyes should never leave your cupped hand. Now imagine that you have dropped it. Respond in movement. Show fear and concern, and with this attitude pick it up. Calm it down without words.

At this point you are to show your audience that the thing you have loved must leave you. It is up to you to decide why it must go. But in your reaction to its leaving, in the way you walk away from it, you will reveal the reason. If it is an unrequited love, your movement will be quite different from one that reflects a parental cutting of apron strings for the child's sake. Decide upon the reason and say it in movement. Be sure your audience can guess it.

Point of View

You have been handed a slip of paper and told that you are to move as the object described on that slip. The slip says, "pen from the point of view of the paper." What would you do? Decide first what the sentence means. You are to communicate the paper's point of view of the pen: how the paper feels about the pen, how the pen affects the paper. It is up to you to imagine the emotions the paper could feel. But in any case you realize that the paper is written upon when flat on a surface, and you do or do not like it.

If your attitude is negative, your stomach will contract. With every stroke of the imaginary pen, your arm, head, leg, or any other

Figure 51

Figure 50

part of your body may move slightly to avoid pain or to express it. The reactions are sharp and heavy. But if you have decided that the pen's actions are the purpose of the paper's life, you would enjoy the writing and express that enjoyment by moving your body slowly, smoothly, indicating what part of your body was being written upon at the moment.

Try both reactions. Find as many variations of movement as you can, always being true to the attitude you wish to project.

When you have worked successfully with the paper and pen, try other concepts, such as: "Tree from the point of view of a leaf"; "cup from the tea's point of view"; "screwdriver as the screw sees it" (Figure 52); "shoe as experienced by the foot." Think first, what is the physical relationship? Then, how does the second object *feel* about the first? Finally, what specific movements would communicate both?

Your next step will be to carry this exercise into human relationships. Act out the master's reaction to the servant, the pupil's reaction to the teacher, the husband's reaction to the wife. Then try acting out the servant as *perceived* by the master, and so on. Finally, portray one character as perceived by several other characters. Or, several characters as they react to one character.

The Thing and Its Shape

Standing alone, straight and motionless, your body has a particular shape. Move it slightly and the form changes enough to change entirely the message it communicated a moment ago. Because your body shape speaks so loudly and varies so greatly with only the slightest change, you, as the actor, must grow conscious of the way certain shapes feel. You cannot rely on your eyes to survey the position you have got yourself into and then report to you the message you have already communicated to your audience. You must *feel* the messages with your muscles.

Let us look at two very distinctive shapes and explore the way they feel when taken on by bodies. First find a dandelion gone to seed. The seeds will fly away when your breath hits them. Let your breath blow them away and watch the particles float and fall, gradually settling onto the grass. Now let your body be a seed. It must be light and wind-touched, and should give a sense of slow time (Figures 53 and 54).

For a completely different body shape, find a heavy but pliable piece of lead wire. With a partner bend it into a distorted, angry form. Look at it and together make your bodies look like the shape you created with the wire. You will feel heavy and angular and quick (Figures 55 and 56).

Pantomime

Here are several exercises that will help you build a world of properties that your audience can visualize. Begin by climbing a ladder. How will you place your hands and feet (Figure 59) so that the audience immediately knows it is a ladder? How will you convince them you are moving upward in space when actually you are remaining in one place? Can you build a little drama around your climbing of the ladder? Perhaps you begin the climb with confidence, happiness, looking up eagerly at your destination. You continue climbing for a very long time, the joy gradually changing to weariness. Suddenly you discover how far above the ground you are. You are petrified. You try to curl yourself around the ladder so you won't fall. You cling for dear life, crying for help (Figure 60). Finally, you are rescued.

Next try a rope. You discover the rope hanging out of the sky. You begin to play with it idly. The rope comes to life. It begins to rise and fall. You watch it with amusement. Then you begin to pull on it. It turns out to be a bell rope, and the tolling of the bell takes you by surprise. You discover the joy of tolling the bell, and you begin pulling the rope harder and faster. Pretty soon it is lifting you off the ground (Figure 61). After a few times, it lifts you too high and you panic and fall. You watch the rope disappear

Figure 52

Figure 53

Figure 54

Figure 55

Figure 56

Figure 57   Figure 58   Figure 59

Figure 60

Figure 61

out of sight. Then it falls again, landing right in your face. In disgust, you get up and leave the rope, casting resentful glances after you. In this pantomime you will want to make particular use of the concept of opposing movements discussed in Chapter VI (*Reaching*).

In this next pantomime you are in a dark room. You walk through space until you bump into an imaginary wall. You explore this wall for a bit until you find another wall perpendicular to it. You become aware that you are in a very oddly shaped room, and you become eager to get out. Where is the door? As you continue to explore the room, you suddenly notice that it is gradually changing shape, quite without warning. You become more desperate to find your way out. The room begins to change shape more quickly. You become panic-stricken and finally exhausted. At last you fall helplessly to the ground, fainting. Fantastic? Ibsen used this situation in *Peer Gynt*, in the scene with the Great Boyg.

You are pulling a boat up on shore. You are holding onto a rope that you keep passing through your hands as the boat nears the shore. Finally you have the boat beached, and you are in the process of tying it up. Out of nowhere a storm comes up and the waves pull the boat back into the water. You engage in a terrible struggle to try to save the boat, but the waves are too strong for you. The rope is pulled through your hands, and finally you have to let go of it, or you will be dragged into the sea. In despair, you watch the boat disappearing in the distance. But the storm becomes worse and worse, and you are forced to take cover. Once again you will need to cultivate opposing movements.

You are trying to launch a raft. You push it down off the beach into the water. Then you try to get onto it. As you get onto it, the raft tips and you fall backward into the water. You try various means of boarding the raft. Finally you are on it, and you try to stand. Again the raft tips. You are forced to lie down on your front and paddle with

your hands. (A related situation is also to be found in *Peer Gynt*.)

You are buying balloons from a balloon man. The balloons are of various sizes and characters. Some of them are plain colors, some have funny faces. As you get more balloons, they begin to pull you upward slightly. Finally you get one balloon too many, and you sail off into the air. You are forced to let go of the balloons, and you sadly watch them disappear.

You have just come home from a hard day of muscular work. You walk into the house and see that your wife is busily packing her summer clothes in boxes. Having a lot to tell her about your day, being proud of your accomplishments in triumphing over great odds, you lean against a pile of boxes and say, with your face only, "Cool it, Baby, Lover Boy is home" (Figure 57). Your wife, however, is singularly uninterested in what you have to say, and before you know it she has you piling one heavy box on top of another one, packing them away in the top of a small closet. You struggle with the boxes. Are you about to destroy the he-man image you just created? Carefully you raise the boxes up (Figure 58), and you have them almost in place when they begin to topple. With gymnastic skill you maneuver them back into place. Satisfied that you have accomplished your task, you turn to embrace your wife when the whole pile of boxes falls off the shelf and knocks you to the floor, unconscious.

You are an Oriental woman whose husband has been killed in a war. His possessions have been returned to you. You unpack them and put them away. Each one brings back a loving memory. Last thing of all is a ceremonial sword. It is beautiful and terrible at the same time. Suddenly the thought occurs to you that if you use the sword on yourself, you can follow your husband. What do you do?

For this next one, let us analyze a little more closely the type of movements that will be used. You are in a box. You have three objectives: (1) to show in movement how large the box is; (2) to communicate your feelings about being there; and (3) to free yourself from the box and express an attitude toward this freedom.

As you create this sketch, you will find that your movements will be of two kinds. The first part of the sketch will require little more than literal movement, pantomime at its simplest. Your hands move along the walls of the box, over the top and across the bottom. This communicates the reality, as we have discussed earlier. It says nothing about your feelings. Because of its literal quality, it is called functional movement. It is the kind of movement you will make greatest use of onstage. Walking, sitting, drinking from a cup, tying a shoe are all functional movements. They get things done; they comprise the business of actual living.

When you begin the second and third parts of the exercise, you may find yourself at a loss. We do not have a prescribed way of relating feelings toward confinement and freedom. You must go back to our discussion of the contraction and release concepts. Explore those movements and find your individual way of telling us what your attitude is toward being trapped and then toward being released. Somewhere within the range defined by *In* and *Out* you will find ways of moving that express this lack of freedom and the recovery of it. Perhaps you are made desperate by it; perhaps you find a sense of security within it. In any case, you can express your reactions by noticing whether they make you feel open or closed or somewhere in between. This kind of movement we call *abstract*.

Abstract movement is just as important onstage as is functional movement. Generally we think of it as belonging to the world of dance, particularly modern dance. When it is used as extensively as you will use it here, it does. We rarely find the actor combining his lines with the kind of movement you used to express your feelings about the box. Nevertheless, the actor uses abstract movement frequently, if often very subtly. For instance, in moments of great anguish, one may "wring" his hands or place his hands over his eyebrows, or in a less familiar way fling his whole body into contortions to match the intensity of the words he is speaking. Certainly, too, the acting that moves into singing and dancing requires a working understanding of the difference between functional and abstract movement. Anyone playing a lead role in a musical comedy must develop a sense of the relationship between words, music, and movement.

Perhaps the most important element in any kind of convincing movement is *motivation*. If you do not know why you are moving, no one else will either. You must have firmly established in your own mind before you move the reason for moving. To practice this, pretend you are entering a room. Your job is to inform the audience, without words, why you entered. Perhaps you are waiting to see a doctor; or perhaps you are checking on a sleeping baby. Find a reason that interests you and move unambiguously. Your audience should have no difficulty guessing your intentions.

Now pretend that you are thumbing, at any speed, through the pages of a book. Convince your audience of your reason.

Take time for exercises such as these to familiarize yourself with the way it feels to know why you are moving. It is essential that you know your character and his situation well enough to know what his motivations are and how he would characteristically reveal them.

To conclude our discussion of movement involving one person, let us look for a moment at the importance of shape. Even unconsciously, we are enormously influenced by the shapes of things; we rely on them for traffic warnings; we are persuaded by their more or less appealing nature into spending money; we worship by them; and we determine our appetites by them. Most fundamentally however, we relate to them kinesthetically. They make us feel certain ways, and we can develop movements to communicate our sensations.

Consider for a moment the circle. This shape falls into many categories of interpretation. In a religious context it symbolizes eternity. In a social context it can represent friendship and steadfastness. But in its endlessness it can also suggest confusion, nondirection, fear. We often unconsciously use the circle to express a state of mind. We pace around the room when worried; we sit in circles for a closer sense of communion. Expressions such as, "I'm running around in circles," or, "My head is spinning," are uttered without thought of their literal meaning.

In both an intellectual and a physical sense, the actor should understand the importance of shapes. As the audience watches you, it will be affected by the shape your body makes in each position you take. It will also be influenced by the general shape of your movements. For example, a sharp zig-zag movement, either in walking or with the hands, might suggest agitation; gently rounded movements might suggest affection; straight lines, anger; wavy lines, sleepiness, and so forth. Even if your character does not positively identify himself with a particular shape as does Dick Deadeye in *Pinafore,* when he says "I'm three-cornered too, ain't I?", you should consider his possible feelings about various shapes and how he might use his body to express them. Think about which ones he would use unconsciously to express himself, and which ones can be worked into the staging and the settings to contribute an additional level of meaning to the production.

Let your imagination go now and consider the ways the circle, for instance, can become a part of your movement vocabulary. Make as many kinds of circles as you can, using various parts of your body. Stand still at first; then let your feet take you in circles around the stage, creating circle upon circle upon circle. Explore the various ways various circles make you feel.

After you have exhausted the possibilities, choose a dramatic scene that interests you and find all the ways in which shape plays a part in the lives of the characters. Become consciously sensitive to shape in this context. You will be able to play the role of any character completely only insofar as you can see and react to the shapes of things and emotions the way he does.

RELATING TO IMAGINARY OTHERS

The Line

In any role you undertake, you will have the problem of deciding how the character feels in one circumstance after another. The majority of your problems will be in your reactions to dialogue; but some reactions, very important ones, will occur in relation to unstated situations. In fact, you will face such reactions and the need to understand them whether you ever do much acting or not.

You have already experienced some unstated relationships. Any time you are a part of a small group of people, you relate to their social standing, their outward appearance, the room you are in, the attitudes they express in the way they sit or stand. Such factors have a tremendous influence on the degree of success you have in communicating with others.

To increase your ability to understand your relationship to unstated situations, be consciously aware of objects, arrangements, colors, clothes, and "categories" of people. When you are standing behind a chair, notice how you feel about it. Is it an obstruction? Do you put your hands on the back of the chair for lack of anything else to do with them? Or is it, perhaps, a thing of sentimental value to you? In addition to this conscious awareness, do the following movement experiment:

Find seven people or seven objects. Place them facing in the same direction in a line. Seat yourself in last position. Sit there until you begin to form or understand your attitude toward being last. Do you feel inferior? Do you have an instructor image? Do you feel hopeless and apathetic, or misplaced and angry? Perhaps you feel ambitious but not vindictive and you aspire to be first. When you have decided what this position means to you, move to express it. Without a word, tell your audience how you feel. You have already worked with movements that could express any one of your reactions. Having become familiar with them, use them. And create new ones.

Giving

Even in our daily lives, giving is very often a wordless thing. Regardless of the form it takes, when it is sincere, it comes from within. The simple gesture of giving a physical object to someone is a motion beginning close to the body and moving outward. To be powerful, the gesture of giving does not have to be grand. It can be done with the fingers alone, and very slowly. Or it can be without hands and arms at all, with any motion that begins within and moves out. Even a chest can move in a giving manner.

Experiment with giving for a moment. First try the simplest form. Imagine a gift in your hands and offer it to someone near. Try it with one hand. Then move from a literal sense to an abstract one and, in as many ways as possible, offer your heart to someone. This can be done with an elbow or a head or a leg. It is the origin of the movement, the sense of beginning from the inside of you, that makes it giving.

Many scenes in your acting career, as well as your daily life, will call for a sincere gesture as an important endorsement of your feelings.

Taking

Just as taking is philosophically the opposite of giving, so it is shown in an opposite way in movement. It begins from without and ends with the focus inward. Explore the concept in movement by finding an object you want in the room. Reach out for it

and take it. Next, assume various attitudes of giving and taking. Find movements similar to those you have already discovered.

Change the dynamics of certain movements: (1) Give willingly. Your walk must aid you. It will need to be sure and yet not aggressive, and your arms will move from your body gradually, steadily outward. (2) Give reluctantly. Your arms may not fully extend, and your walk may be hesitant, your chest turned slightly away from your focus. (3) Give apathetically. With no involvement, the giving will lack arm or body tension. Your pace will be quicker, and your focus should change as soon as the object has been given. (4) Take gently. The movement will be slow, the focus steady. (5) Take angrily. The pace quickens and the arm movement is sharp. Your focus will move as soon as the initial movement is over. (6) Finally, take secretively. Your walk will be unsteady, as will your focus. But the taking will be certain and fast. You will feel light in your movement to the very last moment.

Find four other attitudes for both giving and taking. Try to communicate them to a friend. Move clearly enough to allow him to guess your attitude immediately.

Dialogue in Gesture

In this experiment you will carry on a conversation with a friend purely in gesture. One of you could begin by indicating to the other that he has something to give. The other's reaction, whether through arms raised in surprise or a quick wrist flip in disinterest, will cause the first to react with some particular gesture. You will share reactions without a single spoken word. See how many things you can convey without speaking.

This next exercise involves the use of speech. A speaks to B, perhaps a memorized speech. B responds purely through movement. A adjusts his tone of voice to suit B's response. A thus learns to observe B's movement as a clue to his own performance.

The above exercise is particularly interesting if we apply it to the soliloquy. When you talk to yourself onstage, as in a play of Shakespeare, you are always dividing yourself into two characters. As an exercise, represent these two aspects of the self with two different actors. A, the speaker, asks for, and gets, a response from B, the listener. A, then, will speak the soliloquy to B, who is meant to be the listening side of the self. As B changes his attitude through movement, A's way of speaking must change. Eventually, A should learn to relate to B's physically expressed attitudes. When that happens, his rendering of the soliloquy should become more powerful.

Nonmovement

You have made your body speak. Your arms, chest, legs, head—every part of you has been "heard" in many positions, and with a variety of dynamics. You have learned that whether you are onstage or off, your movement will speak. Exercise and experiment has helped you learn to move so that you have control and command of moving muscles.

Now comes one of the most important results of learning to move: a knowledge of nonmovement. When you understand movement, you have begun to experience the art as well as the difficulty of standing still, of saying nothing. Onstage the actor must be able to stand with his arms at his sides, still and confident. He must know how to move decisively when he moves, and how to keep from moving when nonmovement will best communicate.

The story has frequently been told of Paul Taylor, the dancer, who had such control over his muscles, even his eye muscles, that he succeeded in doing a dance consisting of five full minutes of no movement whatsoever. The curtain opened and he was standing still. By understanding intimately the power of nonmovement, he cast a spell over the audience and held them for five minutes. Silence and stillness can communicate as ef-

fectively as the wildest, most tragic frenzy.

Offstage, too, people speak in nonmovement. Consider, for instance, the young woman who had traveled from her Southern home for a job interview in the North. She had been taught that there is an art to filling in the silence between sections of conversation. To her there was something awkward, unpolished, even insecure in still moments with others. Her background had made her an expert at small talk.

After visiting several offices, she walked into the head office and was greeted cordially by her prospective boss and was seated near his desk. The kind-looking gentleman leaned back in his chair, tapped the arm with the end of his pencil, and said nothing. He looked up. He stopped tapping and smiled slightly. She clutched her hands. Her legs uncrossed and recrossed. She looked at her lap and then into his face and returned the smile. He said nothing and did not move. She could feel her uneasiness, wishing she had no arms or legs.

After ten seconds he said calmly, "Well, what do you think?" Her answer tumbled forth in haste. She explained and reexplained, underlined, and repeated until she could see only a long line of comments behind her, leading nowhere. She ceased talking. He said nothing. Another seemingly endless ten-second silence ensued. Then he asked another question. She found herself babbling again and using gesture and position changes with every phrase. She was exhausted at the end of the interview.

On examination of that encounter, she realized how much self-confidence and polish it takes to sit in complete silence with another person.

Try a moment of silence yourself. Lie on your back with your hands to your sides. Close your eyes. Imagine that you are paralyzed. Paralysis is not stiffness. It is complete immobility. Your legs and arms feel heavy. If you wanted to move them, you could not. Lie with these thoughts and in this position for ten minutes. Keep your thoughts alive, but your body dead.

After you have tried the above exercise, practice standing still. Know that the awkwardness you feel is not sensed by the audience. Strength and self-assurance are communicated in nonmovement. Learn to feel comfortable in the silences.

Chapter XIV

THE SHAPELINESS AND
WEIGHTINESS OF MOVEMENT

Movement has shape. In the pantomime exercises, you were sometimes communicating by creating a sense of the shape of an object you were imagining to exist. You can see from that type of exercise how movement can be used to draw pictures in the air. But movement is always in some sense pictorial, and you will want to develop the ability to sense the general shape of the movement you are creating so that, should the occasion demand it, you will be able to say with the three dragoons in *Patience:*

You hold yourself like this,
You hold yourself like that,
By hook and crook you try to look both an-
    gular and flat.

Do angular movements serve your character best? Or would more circular ones work better? The shape of the movement that typifies your character will have connotations that carry over into other types of experience. A sharp body goes with a sharp tongue, a flat body with the personality that is always falling flat on his face; too graceful a set of circularities in the habits of movement will suggest the superficiality of the water fly.

Movement also has weight. When we say that a motion is heavy, we mean that as the body is moving through space, it is using a certain amount of energy. Weight is to be distinguished from speed or shape. For in-

stance, a very small movement may be heavier than a very large one, and a fast movement may be either weighty or light.

If you have studied a musical instrument, perhaps you will better understand the weight of movement by comparing it to the dynamics of music. Just as you play a note loudly or softly on the piano, so do you move in a relatively loud or soft way. Or perhaps you will find it easier to think of weight as intensity. How strong or weak is the movement? As you familiarize yourself with the weight of movement, you will recognize the fact that through its degree of heaviness, movement communicates in a very precise manner.

Test this fact by choosing an exaggerated gesture and giving it four separate weights. First, make it as light as a five-cent package of potato chips. Pick up the package. Toss it into the air and feel its actual weight with your hands as you catch it. Now transfer that knowledge of weight to your whole body and move as lightly as the package. Increase the speed and size of the same movement without changing its weight. Vary the weight of the movement by picking up next this book, then a table, and finally, a piano (Figure 62). Before you put each object down, be sure you understand the weight of it as it feels in your muscles. Then make your gesture as heavy as the object.

Repeat the four variations, this time vo-

Figure 62

calizing as you do them. You might begin with "Mary Had a Little Lamb." As you let the words and gestures reflect each other, you will discover that words also have weight. When the movement you do is light, your words will probably come forth either in a whisper or in a gently articulated, high-pitched tone. When it is as heavy as the book, you will use a fuller tone emerging from the center of the face. When it reflects the weight of the table, the tone will have a harder, crisper quality. And when the heaviness of the piano is the weight you want, you will use a sound that booms and resonates deep in your chest.

Words also have shape. You can develop your sensitivity to this fact by drawing pictures of the shapes that come to mind when you sound certain words. Compare your drawings with those of someone else who is trying the same experiment. You will find that you can talk about the shape of words and sense that you know what you are talking about.

Speak a sentence and then trace its shape in the air with your finger. Reverse the process: Select a shape and attempt to produce sounds that imitate that shape. Then select objects and attempt to speak in a way that abstracts some quality from the object you have selected, some quality of shape, weight, texture, color, or a combination of these. Try to combine the sounds you make with gestures. Take note of the ways in which gesture and voice work together, reflecting shape and weight.

When you have begun to feel comfortable with this concept, you will be ready to choose a scene from an actual play and examine the ways in which shape and weight characterize the lines as you will say them. Finding shapes that seem to fit your interpretation and vocalizing and moving to reflect them will help to deepen your grasp of the character you are portraying. To expand further your interpretation, you will want to choose shapes and weights at random and arbitrarily superimpose them upon the part. Such random selection will open up new possibilities that you might not otherwise consider.

So far you have worked largely by yourself in attempting to understand the weight and shape of movement and words. But only rarely will you be alone on the stage. Plays are written primarily about the interaction of two or more people, so you will need to discover the weight and shape of movements in which you and someone else are involved. A game you can play will make clear the intricacies of moving and speaking with other actors. You will need six people. There are three parts, two people involved in each part as the other four observe. Begin by getting your body and that of a second person into two interesting patterns. See yourselves as others see you. How do you look to the observers? Then see yourselves not with your eyes or your mind's eye, but with your muscles. Know the shape you are making in space kinesthetically.

Now begin slowly to move. Keep your muscle "eyes" open and feel the difference between the shapes you make. As you are moving, feel the weight of your gesture. Vary the weight as you feel inclined to change your statement. You should be aware of the same elements in the other person. How does the combination of the two bodies say more than only one body? As your friend moves, you should respond to him by moving into a shape and by giving your movement a certain weight that serves as an answer of some kind. Then he will respond in the same way to you. Be keenly aware of the patterns your bodies are making. They should reflect accurately the thoughts in your mind. Allow your movement sketch to reach a peak and come to a conclusion.

A second couple will now repeat the gestures as they saw you and your partner do them, but to the movements they will add words. They will say in dialogue what they think your bodies said in movement. When their sketch is concluded, the third couple will take the scene back into pure gesture, working from the dialogue of the previous sketch and trying to simulate the movement as accurately as possible.

After the three stages have been completed, repeat the scene until each individual has had a chance to play each part. For many reasons it is important for you to act both as a participant and as a spectator in every role in the game. First, as the originator of the idea you will watch the second couple as they interpret your set of movements and translate them into speech. You will see how successful you have been in communicating your basic idea. You will be able to determine whether the shapes you created in space and the weight with which you moved said the things you thought they were saying. Were you accurately seeing yourself as others saw you? Secondly, as you watch the third couple, you will notice the differences between their interpretation of the two sketches and yours. You will notice also the degree to which your basic idea has changed from your original intentions as it passed through the minds and bodies of others. Third, as you move from part to part, you will recognize the problems peculiar to relating gestures to words, and you will see how much easier it is to originate the idea than to interpret and execute someone else's idea. Finally, you will add to your gesture vocabulary by picking up idiosyncratic variations from others.

Another means of building your knowledge of space and weight as they relate to movement and dialogue involves the acting out of an actual scene from a play. Each of the six people works out his own interpretation, concentrating, as before, on the various characteristics of movement and words. After seeing the six interpretations, each of you mirrors the others' movements and copies the tone and inflection and diction of the others' voices. At first you will feel uncomfortable in every interpretation but your own. You should work with the other five variations until you feel at ease with them. You will broaden your range of perform-ance by learning subtle nuances that are outside the range of your habitual means of expression.

Let us look at space and weight from still another angle. Get a group of twenty people together and stand as close to one another as you can. Try to think of togetherness the way a sardine does, lying in its can. How does it make you feel to know that even your breathing and swallowing are sensed by another person? Say something to someone in the group. Experiment with conversations among various members of the group, closely packed together. Now enlarge the space between the group members and carry on more conversations. Expand the group until everyone is three arms' lengths from everyone else. Try some more conversations. Finally, carry on a conversation with someone who is twenty-five feet away from you. Look back over the statements that have been made and notice how they changed—in subject matter, in weight, in accompanying movement.

Now let us get intimate. You want to say "I love you" to your girl friend across the room. How close to her must you be before the circumstances will seem right? Imagine shouting to her from fifty yards away. In fact, take her to the nearest football field and try it. While you are shouting, what are your arms and legs doing? As you move closer, notice the changes. No doubt you will find that the fun increases as the distance decreases.

Next let us try some conversations on the subject of dill pickles. What is in a dill pickle? What, if anything, can be said about dill pickles at zero inches that cannot be said at fifty yards? Give it a try. Notice the elements you choose to work with. For instance, when is the weight of the words more important than the words themselves? How does your accompanying movement vary as you come closer to your partner? Try the discussion with your backs to each other. Then, in the middle of a sentence, turn around, face to face. You will find that there is a lot to be said for the way a dill pickle holds up on such an intimate level.

To conclude our discussion of shape and weight, let us find a means of recording changes in attitude that are brought about by changes in shape. You will need a notebook and a pen. Assume any posture and begin to write a dialogue between two characters, thinking all the time of the shape of your body and of the way the posture you have assumed makes you feel. After several lines are on paper, change your position and continue writing. Make position changes seven or eight times. When you have finished, read over the dialogue. The discontinuities you may find there are caused largely by the movement and feeling changes that occurred in your body. Your posture makes a difference in the way you feel and in the way you interpret the feelings of others.

This explains why grumpy old men are often hunchbacked and dashing young heroes are tall and straight.

Try tying your tie without thinking of shape. Or watch the personality of a sentence sag when the shape and weight of its words are ignored. More drastically, take the concept of these two elements out of society and watch the numbers of unemployed people increase. In one way or another human beings from the beginning of time have built their lives around these two concepts. Columbus discovered America because of them. Man landed on the moon because of them, and your own life is made richer by your increasing awareness and use of them in everything you do. Try breathing without an unconscious dependence upon them. Maybe in your next life you will believe us.

PART IV—IN REHEARSAL AND PERFORMANCE

Chapter XV

BASIC STAGE MOVEMENT

When you are working on the stage in production you have to remember that you are part of a constantly moving picture, and that certain elementary rules govern the effective structuring of that picture. What those rules are depend to some extent on what kind of stage you are working on. We shall consider in this chapter only the proscenium stage and the arena stage.

The proscenium stage is the most common type, being a sort of gigantic box into which the audience looks. Everything that happens on it is seen from about the same point of view. Therefore, the director attempts to prepare a picture that will look best from the approximate center of the audience, while doing nothing that will look very bad from the front, the sides, or the back.

Since all of your audience is on one side of the stage, you will wish to face them as much as possible. It is not a crime to turn your back to the audience, as some people will tell you, but whenever you do so you should have a reason for doing so. Your back will say something very definite that cannot be said with your front.

In order to be sure that we are facing the audiences as much as possible, we learn the concept of upstage and downstage movement. Originally, proscenium stages had floors that slanted upward, away from the audience, so the direction away from the audience is called "upstage," and toward

them, "downstage." If two actors are facing each other onstage, they both "cheat," or face their bodies in about a 45-degree angle downstage. If you wish to cross the stage, you begin and end with the upstage foot. In general, the upstage side of the body should at all times be ahead of its downstage side. When you turn on the stage, you turn toward the audience rather than away from it.

Your position in relation to the other actors is affected by the problem referred to as "upstaging." If you stand in relation to another actor so that he must tend to turn his back to the audience in order to face you, then you are upstaging him. If you do the opposite, forcing yourself to turn your back, then you are upstaging yourself. This means that for the most part actors should play scenes together in about the same plane. It is too easy, however, to become monotonous if one takes this rule literally. The director will vary the action by taking the actors out of the same plane at certain strategic times, but he will quickly get them back together again.

It is annoying to the audience if an actor is blocked from view. If another actor is standing in front of you, it is your responsibility to move so that you can be seen by the audience. You can do so casually and without drawing attention to the action, should it be necessary to move at a time when you are not the focus of attention. Do not simply stand there and let the director worry about the problem; he has more important things to think about.

Movement on the stage has the same kind of shape as movement with the body. You might move in circles or sharp turns. The pattern you make when you move should be associated with the patterns you are using to characterize your part. Many directors will give you the general outline of movement, or "blocking," but most will probably not design all the details, but will leave it to you to determine the exact shape that a movement is to be given. Some directors like to have their actors improvise and to develop the blocking from what they see the actors doing. Your degree of responsibility for the patterns associated with your character may thus vary from one director to another. You are not responsible for the entire stage picture unless you yourself are directing, but you should always be thinking about how your actions may enhance the stage picture created by the director without drawing more attention to your performance than is good for the ensemble.

In relating your performance to that of the other actors, you should bear in mind the importance of upstage and downstage action. For example, if the focus is on you, and you move past another actor, you should move downstage of him. If the focus is not on you, you should move upstage of him. In most cases the focus will be on you, so you should form the habit of passing another actor on the downstage side whenever possible. If two characters embrace and one of them is more important in the play than the other, that one should put his head on the downstage side. If they are of equal importance, the woman's head should be on the downstage side.

Inasmuch as the stage picture must always draw attention to what is most important, no actor should engage in random action while another actor is doing something important. If you are part of a crowd, you should blend into the crowd. If you are carrying on a conversation with someone else that is not to be heard by the audience, while some important action is taking place, you should pantomime the conversation with gestures that are restrained and repetitive—enough to register a conversation, not enough to draw attention to it.

If an important action is happening on one side of the stage and you are not part of it, you should balance the stage by going to the other side if possible. The audience will feel uncomfortable if the characters are not more or less evenly distributed about the stage, unless there is some reason they should not be.

Actors sometimes do a number of distracting things that are annoying to watch. An unconsciously swinging arm is one of the most common. So is the unconscious shifting of weight. Excessive head motion while talking is annoying to watch. Gestures that are too vague or too repetitious should be avoided. In these days of long hair most people are in the habit of brushing their hair out of their eyes or behind their ears quite frequently. This should never happen onstage. Related actions such as scratching oneself or wiping one's nose are also to be avoided, unless they are clearly part of the characterization.

A famous actor once remarked, "You don't stop to pull up your fly when you're dying." If something goes wrong during a dramatic scene, don't worry about it. Carry on as if nothing had happened and let the people backstage figure out what to do. A good scene can be ruined by an actor who is a little too clever in an emergency. Many of the things that will seem like problems to you will go unnoticed by the audience unless you draw attention to them.

You should know how to sit down gracefully. Most people bend over far too much when they sit, and the effect is distracting. Find the edge of the chair with your calves and lower your weight into the chair gradually, using your thighs. Keep your back straight. Do not lean forward unless you are playing a character role.

The above considerations are the primary ones for which you as an actor are responsible. Special kinds of problems will have been thought through by the director. He will expect you to do the things we have discussed here as if they were second nature to you. Nothing annoys a director more than to have to remind an actor not to swing his arm or brush his hair out of his eyes. Some directors are so concerned about the total effect that they ignore such details, assuming that the actors will take care of them on their own.

Let us now consider the problems of movement on an arena stage. In this case the audience is seated entirely around the actors, so there is no upstage and downstage. Instead, the actors must group themselves evenly about the stage and try to handle the action so that it is about as interesting from all points of view. A two-character scene will usually be played at a diagonal, and the actors will switch sides fairly frequently, so that all members of the audience will have adequate exposure to each performer's facial expressions.

A basic rule of acting on the arena stage is that you must learn to act with your back, since 50 percent of the audience is watching your back at all times. This means paying particular attention to how the shoulders reflect emotion. Return to Chapter XI and do the shoulder exercise described there. You want to become as aware of what your shoulders are doing as you are of what your face is doing.

A second basic rule is the use of gestures that tend to lead out from the body circling toward the back. Much more openness of gesture is needed here than on a proscenium stage. Also, if the gestures are above the shoulders they will be visible to everyone.

It is desirable to move in a complete circle whenever possible.

Balancing the stage arena style means avoiding straight lines. Actors should make use of the greater freedom of dimensionality by forming triangles, squares, circles, and irregular figures. Upstaging is never any problem.

It is important to keep your head up whenever you are performing on the stage. A head that is bent forward directs the voice to the floor rather than to the audience. The face is likely to be covered with shadows, as most of the lighting comes from above. In an arena stage, however, the audience is more likely to be above you than below you, and so it is even more important to keep your head up and perhaps even slightly back. The higher your head is held, the more people will be able to see your face.

Most other types of stage combine aspects of the arena and proscenium stage. If you have mastered the techniques appropriate to each of them, you will be able to make the necessary adaptations when working on another kind of stage.

To summarize, we have pointed out in this chapter a number of the things that should be habitual in your behavior as an actor. The director will have much to say about your physical performance and will help you solve the special problems that arise in a given play. If you have to fight a duel, for example, you will probably have a fencing coach. If stabbing is called for, the director will know the best way to do it. Your responsibility is to avoid annoying him with bad habits that can easily be corrected, and to show him that you are well versed in the rudiments of stage technique so that he never has to go over routine matters in working with you. If you do not exhaust him with trivia, he will be far better able to help you achieve an exciting performance.

Chapter XVI

BREAKING THE HAM BARRIER

When you read a play and imagine how it should be performed, everything is happening inside your head. Your mind becomes a stage on which all the characters act, each of them to perfection. You imagine yourself as all of the characters and are able to achieve any effect you desire. When you participate in an actual performance, the play that has been inside your head must be transferred thence to inside the heads of the members of the audience. What has been so real and alive and subtle in your imagination must be exaggerated a hundredfold. That is by no means an easy task. It will seem, at first, very unnatural. For one thing, you will have to accept the fact that you can never speak and move on the stage as you do in real life. You must always speak louder and move in a way that is both exaggerated and purified, in that no excessive, unwanted action is performed. That may seem like hypocrisy to you, and if the slightest hint of hypocrisy in anything frightens you, the theatre is perhaps not for you. "It isn't me," you will think, as you do what is required to project your personality to an audience. If you think that, you are forgetting that the audience is not sitting inside your head and cannot possibly see what you see there. Do not think of projection as hypocrisy, think of it as translation. You are translating your thoughts from the special language in which they occur inside your head into another language that can be understood at a distance. The translation involves making everything larger than life—more frightening, more beautiful, more energetic. You will have to exaggerate everything you do to be successful (Figure 63).

Every good actor begins by being a ham. A ham actor is one who puts more into a performance than an audience feels is effective. He overdoes everything so much that the effect is irritatingly artificial, and sometimes embarrassing. Ham acting is pure exaggeration. Good acting, on the other hand, is exaggeration tempered by artistic judgment. Ham acting provides the raw material from which good acting may be made. Until you are willing to go through the process of giving a performance everything you've got regardless of the consequences, you cannot develop the resources that will make you a good actor.

Your problem is to break down the barrier of reticence that prevents you from being a ham actor. There is no particular technique for doing this; what is required is will power. You decide that you are going to exhaust your physical and emotional capacity in the performance of a role. In doing so you open up vast reserves that you had never dreamed you possessed. You use wider, more frequent, more rapid gestures, and a much louder voice fraught with intense emotion. It is the authors' experience that most amateur actors when told to exaggerate to the point of ridiculousness will end by doing something just barely adequate in terms of projection. What seems to them excessive is, from an audience's point of view, absolutely minimal. They are actors

138

Figure 63

who have not yet dipped into the tremendous emotional reserves on which they can draw by breaking the ham barrier.

If you have made up your mind to put your performance across, begin by being dissatisfied with everything you do. Play a scene so powerfully that you are physically and emotionally exhausted by the experience, and while you are lying on the floor recovering, tell yourself, "That was only one tenth of what I need to do." Do not begin to be satisfied until others have noticed a significant change in your acting. If, after your best efforts, the director is still telling you to speak louder, and you still feel that people are not really watching what you do, you must once more redouble your efforts.

When you have broken the ham barrier, you will know it. When you perform, everyone will pay attention. You will not necessarily get favorable reactions to your acting, but you will get clearly stated ones. If it happens in rehearsal, the director will start telling you to speak more softly or to use more restraint. If it happens in acting class, there will be a certain kind of excitement about what you are doing. Your fellow students will be seeing something new from you. They and your teacher may react with either applause or criticism or some combination of the two, but they will not react as they have before. If it happens in performance, you will sense that the audience is more responsive than previously. You may find out afterward that the more sophisticated members of the audience were skeptical, but that the children loved it.

Breaking the ham barrier is an important step in any actor's life. He should feel victorious at having conquered his reticence and opened up new territory in his artistic resources. He should not feel guilty or allow himself to be discouraged by criticism. He should continue to act exuberantly and allow himself the luxury of unstinted exuberance for a while before he becomes too concerned with artistic control.

But a time will come when control must be developed. You should not become the type of actor who measures his success by the amount of noise the audience makes in response to him. Good acting is subtle and often measured by the degree of silence in a listening audience. Do not become one of those who thrive on the noisy reactions of the vulgar while the critical remain coldly silent. Do not assume that it is *always* desirable to get a laugh. Above all, do not assume that if an audience responds to something you do, you should immediately do more of it. After intensity must come a certain lightness and relaxation. All great actors are relaxed, saving the intensity for the grand climax. The less experienced actor uses all his energies in the first scene and then has nothing with which to build.

Ham acting is like unmodeled clay waiting to be shaped, to be given form, texture, subtlety. The assurance that you can always do more lies behind the intricacy and control of what you are doing. It is the ever present energy that guarantees that you will be able to continue and thus protects you like the net below the trapeze artist. It is the vast pool of energy from which you draw the small part that serves the needs of the moment. It is the foundation for relaxation and naturalness.

Have we come full circle? We started with the naturalness inside the head and argued that there is no place for it on the stage. Now we speak of the naturalness that lies beyond ham acting. There is no contradiction. Once you have become an experienced actor you will be so skilled at translating what is inside your head into a theatrical language that an audience can understand that you will even have fooled yourself. The highly exaggerated intensification and selection from real life that appears so natural on the stage will also seem natural to you. No longer will you have to think about projection; you will have begun to live the part.

Chapter XVII

CHARACTER BASE

One of the techniques sometimes used by the oil painter is to apply layers of paint of various colors. The layer on the surface will determine the actual color that the eye sees, but the layers beneath will shine through, giving the surface color a quality it could not achieve by itself. This technique may be used to illuminate a face in a portrait so that it seems to have a character that emanates from within. Certainly it gives the painting a richness and complexity that could be achieved in no other way.

People also develop in layers. The process of growing up involves trying out various character traits and behavior patterns until one achieves those that seem most comfortable under the circumstances and will be retained throughout life. The earlier qualities may be forgotten, but they are not lost. They remain to shine through, subtly influencing the behavior of one's maturity. The seductress was once a shy little wallflower. The prudish old man sowed his wild oats in his youth. The narrow-minded conservative of today was the free-thinking radical of yesterday. The dry philosopher was as a child given to temper tantrums.

How do past characteristics shine through in the present? That would be difficult to say. Perhaps there occur occasional lapses into former ways. Perhaps one works a little extra hard at being what one is in order to avoid being what one was. It may be that one is a little overeager for reassurance that

he has indeed escaped the excesses of the past. Or one may condemn in others what he has learned to dislike in himself. The shining-through will always be difficult to pinpoint, but it will be there nonetheless. There will be sensuality lurking behind the brittleness of the prudish voice. The elegance of the graceful lady will occasionally give a hint of the tomboy that she once was.

In building your character you will want the richness and subtlety of a fully dimensioned personality, not merely the character that is shown on the surface. If your character has had to struggle to make himself what he is, spend some time acting out what he once was. Then build his present behavior patterns on top of the earlier ones. If you are portraying the nagging wife, act out the love scenes that preceded the marriage so that you can let the audience feel what the character has lost. If you are old and crippled, build your age on top of the youth you once had. As you move, recall how much easier things were in the past and feel all the more forlorn.

It is wise to approach rehearsals from the point of view that you are going to find your character by degrees. If you are an old man, do not hobble through the first rehearsal. Play the lines with youthful vigor, making sure that you understand the emotions behind them, and then age them by degrees. Never go for the superficial qualities first; let them come in good time. Begin with the

141

Figure 64

humanness of your character and work into his specialness. Work out logically the stages of physical behavior in the development of your character. Try many possible faces on him (Figure 64).

Character base is largely a physical matter. You want to achieve an understanding of your character's posture, of the way he walks, of the kind of arm movements that characterize him. You want to assume the general vocal quality that he would use. You want to get into his body and feel comfortable there. Remember that he feels his emotions in terms of his body, not in terms of yours. Sir Laurence Olivier put it beautifully when he said, "I usually collect a lot of details, a lot of characteristics, and find a creature swimming about somewhere in the middle of them." He went on to observe, "The actor who starts from the inside is more likely to find himself in the parts he plays, than to find the parts in himself."

As an exercise to help you understand the development of character in layers, select a fairly long speech in a play and work at it in the following way. Begin by deciding what physical characteristics are appropriate to the speech. Act it out using those characteristics. Then decide what physical characteristics are exactly opposite to the ones you have previously worked with. Act the speech again, with the opposing characteristics. Now return to the original characteristics, but retain the others in the background. Act the character in such a way that he is repressing his opposite characteristics. Experiment with increasing and decreasing the tension between the two sets of characteristics. Experiment with various ways of playing one against the other. In one case, feel that you are physically suppressing actual urges. In another case feel somewhat wistful that you cannot be the opposite of what you are. In a third case, lapse now and then ever so slightly into the opposite behavior. In a fourth case, concentrate on feeling deep-rooted contempt for the opposite behavior.

Now ask yourself another kind of question about the characterization: not what is opposite, but what most probably immediately preceded the present stage of development. For example, if you are playing Hamlet you will switch from the moody, introspective character revealed in the play to the dashing, chivalrous character that we are told preceded it. You will play Hamlet in the latter way and then superimpose the former characterization on top of it.

We have suggested this sequence of exercise because it is always easier to think in terms of opposites than more subtle differences. Get the idea of superimposing one layer on another first, then make the layers more closely interrelated. Finally, work with more than two layers, eventually progressing to four or five.

In your study of literature you have probably become used to distinguishing between the literal or "surface" meaning of a poem or story and the symbolic or "deep" meaning. Good art of all kinds exists on more than one level of expression. It may not have occurred to you before that good acting can work in the same way. You will begin to achieve interesting, subtle, and perhaps even great performances when you can let a variety of levels shine through to the surface of your character in such a way that you make a statement about the character that is simple and clear and at the same time rich with undercurrent realities. Do not neglect the surface. It must be very strong. But its strength can wait until the final rehearsals to crystallize. Earlier, you are dissecting the character, discovering the anatomy of his emotions and movement, continually fascinating yourself with his extraordinary complexity as a human being. Let your own fascination become the source of fascination for your audience.

Chapter XVIII

YOUR FUTURE AS AN ACTOR

It takes at least ten years to make a good actor. The constant molding and remolding, examination and reexamination of every phase of performance that finally produces a recognizable acting style is an extraordinarily complex process. Your personal style will grow out of gradually getting to know yourself as an actor—what you do poorly as well as what you do well, what emotions you best express, how you typically affect an audience, above all, how you look.

Let us distinguish between personal style and individual characterization. You may perform many expert characterizations before you develop your own style. There is something about an expert professional actor that makes one look forward to seeing him in whatever part he does. Something of the actor's personality will be inextricably entwined with the individual characteristics of the role he is playing. One will never lose the role, but one will always sense the actor through it and marvel at the instruments that are his body and his voice. No matter how brilliant a performance you may give, you will not make anyone particularly want to see you again until you have developed your own style.

You cannot do much during the earlier stages of your development to hasten the process. Indeed, you should not try to hasten it. Your style will come when it is ready to, and attempting to fasten onto something prematurely would only limit you. On the other hand, before you have developed your style you are in a much better position to affect the quality of what you will eventually achieve than you will be later. The early stages of development lay the foundation for what is to come and they may spell success or failure.

Stinting yourself on the fundamentals of speech and movement may cost you the career you dream of. You should learn good diction at the very beginning. You should learn proper breathing habits. You should cultivate good posture. You should improve your walking. Daily exercise of the right kind is extremely important in laying a proper foundation. It would be a good idea for you to begin as soon as possible to work out a schedule for daily exercise that touches on each of the essentials discussed in this book. Make a schedule like the one that follows in the Appendix and attempt to stick to it. It is too much to ask to expect you to exercise every day, but five times a week is most desirable; and if you are exercising fewer than three times a week you need to reconsider your schedule.

Ideally you should work with an instructor who can guide you in making out your schedule and criticize you from time to time in the way you are doing the exercises, as well as help you decide which exercises are most important for you. If it is not possible at this time for you to receive acting instruction, however, that should not deter you from accomplishing what you can on your own. Many of the finest actors have largely trained themselves, in the early stages at least. The important thing to realize is that exercise has a more powerful effect the younger you are, and every day that goes by without exercise represents a reduction in the quality that you will eventually be able to achieve.

Whenever you work with a particular production you help to set the habits that will eventually determine your style. It is most damaging to practice a bad habit. The powerful effect of performance is such that a bad habit practiced during a performance receives about ten times as much reinforcement as a bad habit practiced during a rehearsal. Therefore, unless you are actively working to improve your basic techniques, opportunities to play leading roles are not necessarily going to benefit you. They may even prove harmful.

You will be better able to stick to your schedule of exercise and receive more benefits from it if you are highly motivated. You will probably not become a successful actor unless you want to very much. If you do not want to cultivate acting as more than a hobby, then you can experiment casually with the exercises in this book, realizing that you will get some benefits from whatever you do with them, benefits that will frequently carry over from your enjoyment of acting into other areas, such as personal poise, success in dealing with people, and a general feeling of well-being.

If, on the other hand, you do wish to become a successful professional actor, you should spend plenty of time thinking about both the positive and negative aspects of such a career. On the positive side, there is probably nothing more exhilarating than giving a truly great performance for an appreciative audience while working with other competent actors. The highly skilled professional actor experiences life on a plane that is inaccessible to even the most enthusiastic amateur. There is a certainty of excellence in much of what he does that makes all the sacrifices necessary to achieve success seem

entirely worthwhile. The excitement of working with other good actors is something that must be experienced to be appreciated.

On the negative side, the chances for success are very small because of the tremendous competition. Even the best actor may fall by the wayside because he does not happen to be in the right place at the right time in order to get the part that will make him famous. At any given time, 93 percent of all professional actors are unemployed. Much of the work that is available is tedious. Many actors make television commercials or appear in small parts in soap operas or educational films. The creative actor remains undaunted by even the dullest material, feeling that it is always a challenge to try to bring it to life. One should not have illusions about the likelihood of immediate fame and fortune.

If you are to be successful against the enormous amount of competition you will face, you must work very hard, particularly at the basic exercises. You will need to bring yourself to a professional level of performance before you can expect to do any professional acting. This means driving yourself hard for a long time. It does not mean driving yourself so hard that you collapse. You must find a pace you can maintain without jeopardizing your health and happiness, and then maintain it.

People who are successful have certain common characteristics in the way they approach tasks. They adjust their goals to the immediate reality that surrounds them. They have long-range goals, but they are very much aware of what is necessary in taking the next step. They do not try to skip steps in their development.

The successful person is a moderate risk taker. If there is a good chance that he will succeed at something, he will try it. If success is highly unlikely, he will not be interested. Nor will he be interested in anything that does not represent a challenge to him. He will undertake relatively difficult tasks and feel that it is very important that he be successful at them. In order to achieve success more effectively, he will carefully analyze the things that stand in his way. Some of them will be problems that lie within his own character, things he can change if he works at them. Some of them will be obstacles that lie outside his immediate control, which must be surmounted if he wishes to achieve success. He will thus select his tasks in the light of the obstacles that must be overcome to achieve success.

The successful person is always open to suggestion. He never resents help or advice from others. He knows that anything that helps him to be more successful is of value, and so he does not let possible hurt feelings get in the way of seeking out and receiving help. Consequently, the successful person attempts to surround himself with people who are wiser, more experienced, and more skilled than he is. That will provide him with the most opportunities to learn. He is

never concerned with how good he is in relation to other members of the group, only in relation to his own previous performance. He has his own standards and maintains them no matter what circumstances surround him. He is always competing with himself against a standard of excellence.

If you will adopt the qualities of the successful man in your own personality, you will greatly improve your chances of achieving the goal you have set for yourself. If someday you become a successful actor it will not be because of what happens in the future alone. Your success will depend to a very large extent on what happens *now*. As you work on the exercises in this book, you are laying the foundation stones for a personal style that may someday make millions of people want to spend their evenings being fascinated by you. Lay those stones carefully.

APPENDIX

* If you are jogging.
** If you are doing Aerobics you may do only the calesthenics, and thus reduce your time here by several minutes.

IV.   IDEAS IN MOVEMENT (TIME VARIABLE)

V.   GROUP EXERCISES

Books on Acting, Theatre and Dance

Albright, H. D. *Working Up a Part*. Boston: Houghton Mifflin Company, 1959. A brief treatment of movement, speech, and characterization, helpful to the beginner.

Anderson, Virgil A. *Training the Speaking Voice*. New York: Oxford University Press, 1942. One of the best books available on the technique of voice production, it offers a complete technical explanation of the vocal apparatus and the best means of using it.

Appia, Adolphe. *The Work of Living Art* and *Man Is the Measure of All Things*. Coral Gables: University of Miami Press, 1960. Although intended primarily for set designers, this book has some abstractions on living time, space, and color that may appeal to the actor interested in his relation to the total stage picture.

Armstrong, Margaret. *Fanny Kemble: A Passionate Victorian*. New York: Macmillan, 1938. A biography of a great nineteenth-century actress who was equally at home in comedy and tragedy. A good picture of the theatre and society of the time.

Berne, Eric. "Notes on Games and Theatre," *Tulane Drama Review,* Summer, 1967. The author of *Games People Play* analyzes dramatic situations in terms of the hidden motives that characters use in manipulating one another.

Blakelock, Denys. *Advice to a Player*. London: William Heineman, Ltd., 1958. Practical advice on auditioning and job-hunting intended for the British actor.

Blau, Herbert. "A Subtext Based on Nothing," *Tulane Drama Review,* Winter, 1963. Discussion of a production of *King Lear* in which the problem of relating Shakespeare's situations and the inner experiences of the actor is creatively dealt with.

Blunt, Jerry. *Stage Dialects*. San Francisco: Chandler Publishing Company, 1967. The fundamental information necessary for learning eleven dialects is here. Recorded tapes designed to accompany the book are also available.

Boleslavsky, Richard. *Acting: The First Six Lessons*. New York: Theatre Arts Books, 1939. The emphasis here is on training the actor's imagination. Boleslavsky's work with the Moscow Art Theatre gave him an excellent background in the techniques originated by Stanislavsky.

Bowman, Walter Parker, and Robert Hamilton Ball. *Theatre Language: a Dictionary of Terms in English of the Drama and Stage from Medieval to Modern Times*. New York: Theatre Arts Books, 1961. More than 3,000 words and phrases used in connection with the theatre are defined here.

Boyle, Walden P. *Central and Flexible Staging: A New Theater in the Making*. Berkeley: University of California Press, 1956. This contains valuable information on how to adapt productions to various types of stage.

Brown, John Russell. "Marlowe and the Actors," *Tulane Drama Review,* Summer, 1964. This article provides many insights on how to act Marlowe as well as other flamboyant classics.

Bryant, Donald C., and Karl R. Wallace. *Oral Communication: A Short Course in Speaking*. New York: Appleton, Century Crofts, 1962. This book deals with public speaking and oral interpretation. It includes many exercises useful in the development of good voice production.

Burton, Hal (ed.). *Great Acting*. New York: Hill and Wang, 1967. A large, beautiful book containing magnificent photographs and penetrating interviews with leading British actors.

Chaikin, Joseph. "The Actor's Involvement: Notes on Brecht," *The Drama Review,* Winter, 1968. Brecht's ideas about alienation are dealt with as an acting problem.

Chaplin, Charles. *My Autobiography*. New York: Simon and Schuster, 1964. The greatest of the silent film stars tells how he rose to fame, how he developed his style, and how he dealt with the personal setbacks he had to face.

Cohen, Selma Jean (ed.). *The Modern Dance: Seven Statements of Belief*. Middletown: Wesleyan University Press, 1966. This collection provides a unique experience with the thinking of seven world-famous dancers and choreographers. These artists deal with the common subject of "The Prodigal Son," explaining how they would choreograph it, and revealing their personal attitudes toward dance creation. The artists are José Limón, Anna Sokolow, Erick Hawkins, Donald McKayle, Alwin Nikolais, Pauline Korner, and Paul Taylor.

Cole, Toby (ed.). Acting: *A Handbook of the Stanislavski Method*. New York: Lear, 1947. A number of leading lights in the Moscow Art Theater offer comments on various aspects of the art of acting.

──────, and Helen Krich Chinoy (eds.). *Actors on Acting*. New York: Crown Publishers, 1949. More than 100 actors and writers explain in their own words their theories about acting.

──────. *Directing the Play: A Source Book of Stagecraft*. Indianapolis: Bobbs-Merrill, 1953. Contains an introductory chapter on the emergence of the director and articles by leading directors of the nineteenth and twentieth centuries.

Corry, Percy. *Amateur Theatrecraft*. London: Museum Press, Ltd., 1961. Good, if you're a complete beginner and don't want to be burdened with too many specifics.

Craig, Edward Gordon. *Henry Irving*. London: J. M. Dent, 1930. An idolatrous portrait of the great nineteenth-century actor by a man who has greatly influenced modern stage design.

De Mille, Agnes. *Dance to the Piper*. Boston: Little, Brown, 1952. A beautifully written autobiography by the choreographer, dancer, and comedienne who rose to fame with *Oklahoma!* The plight of the American dancer in the early years of this century is clearly portrayed, as is the rigorous training of the dancer and a highly personal view of Martha Graham.

Diderot, Denis. *The Paradox of Acting,* and Archer, William. *Masks or Faces?* New York: Hill and Wang, 1957. An analysis of the actor's basic creative processes grows out of this theoretical discussion developed in two classic and conflicting documents.

Dolman, John, Jr. *The Art of Play Production*. New York: Harper, 1928. Considers acting problems in the context of play rehearsal. Contains a brief summary of the Diderot-Archer controversy.

Duerr, Edwin. *Radio and Television Acting*. New York: Rinehart, 1950. Concentrates heavily on microphone techniques, and is somewhat outdated.

Easty, Edward Dwight. *On Method Acting*. New York: Allograph Books, 1966. Quite different in approach from our book, this stresses sense and affective memory in the creation of a character's inner life. Particularly interesting are the animal exercises.

Fast, Julius. *Body Language*. New York: M. Evans, 1970. This is a popularized treatment of a subject that is still in the early stages of research. Much of it is very general, but there are a few specifics that may be helpful to the actor attempting physical characterization.

Feldenkrais, Moshe, "Image, Movement, and Actor: Restoration of Potentiality," *Tulane Drama Review,* Spring, 1966. A judo expert discusses acting in terms of physical control and shows that there is a close connection between the operation of mind and body.

Fowler, Gene. *Good Night, Sweet Prince: The Life and Times of John Barrymore.* New York: Viking, 1944. One of the finest biographies of actors, this gives a largely anecdotal account of Barrymore's career.

Funke, Lewis, and John E. Booth. (eds.). *Actors Talk About Acting.* New York: Random House, 1961. Fourteen interviews with contemporary actors that give each actor an opportunity to express his views at some length.

Gassner, John. *Producing the Play.* New York: Holt, Rinehart & Winston, 1953. A valuable anthology of essays on all aspects of production. Lee Strasberg's article on acting offers a good introduction to American "method" acting.

Gielgud, John. *Stage Directions.* New York: Random House, 1963. Informal essays, largely autobiographical, helping to develop a sense of what works in the theatre.

Goodman, Edward. *Make Believe: The Art of Acting.* New York, Scribner's, 1956. Lively both in style and content, this book must take second place to the great Russian and British schools. Detailing the methods of Charles Jehlinger of the American Academy of Dramatic Arts, it is representative of the traditional American approach to acting.

Gorchakov, Nikolai M. *Stanislavski Directs.* New York: Funk & Wagnalls, 1954. A wide range of dramatic styles is covered in this eyewitness account of a great director at work.

Hanley, Theodore D., and Wayne L. Thurman. *Developing Vocal Skills.* New York: Holt, Rinehart & Winston, 1962. Concerned entirely with voice production, this book offers a good technical background for understanding the excellent exercises it contains.

Harrison, G. B. *Elizabethan Plays and Players.* Ann Arbor: Ann Arbor Books, 1956. A scholarly discussion of the theatre of Shakespeare's time and the playwrights and actors who made it what it was.

Hartnoll, Phyllis (ed.). *The Oxford Companion to the Theatre.* New York: Oxford, 1951. One of the best reference books on all phases of theatre.

H'Doubler, Margaret N. *Dance: A Creative Art Experience.* Madison: The University of Wisconsin Press, 1968. A thorough, beautifully written discussion of dance as an expression of the innermost impulses of man. The work includes a cultural survey of dance, an analysis of the creative urge and its application to form. Perhaps the single most vital work dealing with dance.

Hobbs, William. *Techniques of the Stage Fight: Swords, Firearms, Fisticuffs and Slapstick.* New York: Theatre Arts Books, 1967. A beautiful, detailed treatment with plenty of illustrations. Covers every aspect of the subject, including battle scenes.

Humphrey, Doris. *The Art of Making Dances.* New York: Grove Press, 1959. An exquisitely written discussion on choreography useful to both teacher and student. One of the world's finest and most famous dancers and choreographers weaves the feeling and power of the dance into a lucid and helpful series of chapters on the teaching of dance choreography. The book is well illustrated.

Hunt, Douglas and Kari. *Pantomime: The Silent Theater.* New York: Atheneum, 1964. *Very* sketchy from the actor's point of view. Mostly history. A number of good photos.

Jones, Margo. *Theatre-in-the-Round.* New York: Rinehart and Company, 1951. One of the leaders in the arena stage movement writes a fuller and more specific book than Boyle's. Fifteen pages on acting.

Joseph, Bertram. *Acting Shakespeare*. New York: Theatre Arts Books, 1963. An investigation of Shakespeare's background in learning to write plays leads to some helpful information on how to act Shakespeare for contemporary audiences so as to reveal the rich verbal structure of the plays.

——————. *Elizabethan Acting*. New York: Oxford, 1951. The student interested in theories of acting and rhetoric of the past will enjoy this book. Particularly fascinating are the illustrations of rhetorical gestures of the hand taken from John Bulwer's *Chirologia and Chironomia,* 1644.

——————. *The Tragic Actor*. New York: Theatre Arts Books, 1959. A history of English tragic acting with specific reference to the great tragic actors and helpful information for the contemporary actor.

Joseph, Stephen. *Theatre in the Round*. London: Barrie and Rockliff, 1967. Somewhat amateurish by comparison with Margo Jones's book, it tends to be unspecific about arena acting problems.

Kahan, Stanley. *Introduction to Acting*. New York: Harcourt, Brace and World, 1962. A textbook for college acting classes with emphasis on the technical side of acting.

Kirby, E. T. *Total Theater, A Critical Anthology*. New York: E. P. Dutton, 1969. A collection of historical and philosophical essays dealing with the theatre as an "intersection of all the arts." The student will find it interesting to form his own opinions as to the place the actor holds in this concept. There are valuable discussions and historical documentations of actual productions of Vakhtangov, Craig, Appia, Wagner, and of Chinese and Kabuki theatre. The essay on music and dance in the productions of Max Reinhardt is particularly relevant to our study of movement.

Kirby, Michael. *Happenings*. New York: E. P. Dutton, 1965. A collection of statements about and scripts of Happenings, with an interesting introduction defining the Happening as it exists separately from the other arts. One realizes from this comprehensive, vivid picture that the structured nonstructure of the Happening gives it a validity all its own. There is much meat here for the student of nonverbal theatre.

Lawson, Joan. *Mime*. New York: Pitman, 1957. A somewhat tedious but informative discussion of basic body gestures, emphasizing the details of many ballet positions. Contains a section on characterization in which the author traces the development of various characters purely through movement.

Lees, C. Lowell. *A Primer of Acting*. New York: Prentice-Hall, 1940. A clear, easily understood book for the beginner, containing a number of excellent exercises.

Lewes, George Henry. *On Actors and the Art of Acting*. New York: Grove Press. Some of the best late nineteenth-century dramatic criticism with observations of leading actors from Kean to Salvini and an essay, "On Natural Acting."

Lewis, Mary Kane. *Acting for Children*. New York: John Day, 1969. Designed to be used with young children and very basic, this book maintains a good balance between technique, improvisation, and pantomime.

Marash, J. G. *Mime in Class and Theatre*. London: Harrap, 1950. Some good pointers in the opening chapters, together with many ideas for produceable mimes. Somewhat artificial in its approach.

Marowitz, Charles. *Stanislavsky and The Method*. New York: Citadel, 1961. Historical and critical in approach, this book places Stanislavsky in the perspective of the modern theatre and relates his techniques to the production of Shakespeare and Brecht.

Martin, John. *The Modern Dance*. New

York: Dance Horizons, 1968. A series of lectures forming one of the first books to attempt an explanation of modern dance, this is an exciting philosophical look at the art.

Matthews, Brander. *On Acting.* New York: Scribner's, 1914. A short, general account of acting in the abstract intended as an introduction. Includes interesting material on actors such as Garrick, Booth, and Joseph Jefferson.

——————— (ed.). *Papers on Acting.* New York: Hill and Wang, 1958. Of more interest to the historian than the acting student, this offers the views of a number of pre-twentieth century actors. By no means as complete as Cole and Chinoy.

Melville, Harald. *Theatrecraft: The A to Z of Show Business.* London: Rockliff, 1954. A helpful introduction to all phases of professional work in theatre, written from a British point of view.

Moffett, James. *Drama: What Is Happening.* Illinois: National Council of Teachers of English, 1967. A brief discussion of the value of soliloquy, monologue, and dialogue in the teaching of literature. Moffett maintains that an experiential approach to concepts results in more personalized learning.

Moore, Sonia. "The Method of Physical Actions," *Tulane Drama Review,* Summer, 1965. Amplification of the idea developed in her book on Stanislavsky, presented in the form of a series of questions and answers.

——————— . *The Stanislavski System.* New York: Viking, 1965. A short and simple explanation, which makes a good introduction to Stanislavsky's own books.

——————— . *Training an Actor.* New York: The Viking Press, 1968. A series of transcriptions of acting classes including a number of valuable exercises.

Morris, Robert. "Notes on Dance," *Tulane Drama Review,* Winter, 1965. An approach to movement that uses objects as a means of creating new structures in body movement. Anti-traditional and exploratory in outlook.

Munk, Erika. *Stanislavski and America.* New York: Hill and Wang, 1966. An anthology of essays from the *Tulane Drama Review* containing many varied views of "method" acting.

Nagler, A. M. *Shakespeare's Stage.* New Haven: Yale University Press, 1958. A scholarly discussion of the physical aspects of Shakespeare's theatre, potentially helpful to the would-be Shakespearean actor.

Nelms, Henning. *Play Production.* New York: Barnes & Noble, 1950. A comprehensive and easily available handbook on all phases of play production, particularly useful for the actor who wishes to be aware of those phases of production in which he has not been trained.

Newman, Frank. *The Producer and the Actor.* London: J. Garnet Miller, 1951. Basic principles of work, designed for amateurs.

Newton, Robert G. *Together in Theatre.* London: J. Garnet Miller, 1950. How working together effectively can improve the production. Exercises in listening, playing in the scene, keeping in the picture, projection, and tension.

Ommaney, Katharine Anne. *The Stage and the School.* New York: McGraw-Hill, 1960. A textbook that covers all phases of theatre and contains a number of scenes for several actors, as well as useful appendices, including one on considering a theatrical career.

Oxenford, Lyn. *Design for Movement.* London: J. Garnet Miller, 1953. Stage movement for individuals and crowds with emphasis on the differing demands of various types of plays.

——————— . *Playing Period Plays.* London: J. Garnet Miller, 1955. Published in several small volumes, these books are written with insight and give practical pointers on how to handle English plays from the Middle Ages to recent times.

Paris, Robert Graham. *How to Act.* New

York: Harper, 1959. Written in a relaxed, entertaining style, this book covers the basic techniques in as painless a manner as possible.

Pearson, Hesketh. *Beerbohm Tree: His Life and Laughter*. New York: Harper, 1956. One of the leading theatrical figures of the late nineteenth century is revealed in a highly entertaining biography.

Pickersgill, M. Gertrude. *Practical Miming*. London: Pitman, 1957. This little book may be hard to find, but it's full of good specific suggestions on mime technique, if you don't take its dated philosophy too literally.

Price, Julia S. *The Off-Broadway Theater*. New York: The Scarecrow Press, 1962. A history of the movement, possibly helpful to an actor seeking work in off-Broadway theatre.

Redfield, William. *Letters from an Actor*. New York: Viking Press, 1967. These letters were written during the production of Richard Burton's *Hamlet*, and reflect the inner workings of that production as seen by an actor playing one of the lesser roles.

Redgrave, Michael. *The Actor's Ways and Means*. New York: Theatre Arts Books, 1953. A classic book on acting by one of Britain's finest actors.

——————. *Mask or Face*. New York: Theatre Arts Books, 1958. A collection of essays and reminiscences.

Rockwood, Jerome. *The Craftsmen of Dionysus: An Approach to Acting*. New York: Scott, Foresman, 1966. Emphasis on the psychology of acting. Contains many useful and imaginative exercises.

Rogoff, Gordon. "The Actor as Private Man," *Tulane Drama Review*, Summer, 1963. This article discusses the problems of an actor who is concerned with developing integrity as an artist.

Ross, Lillian and Helen. *The Player, a Profile of an Art*. New York: Simon and Schuster, 1962. Interviews with contemporaray actors have provided the basis for a large number of short articles telling how they feel about acting.

Schyberg, Frederik. "The Art of Acting: What is an Actor?" *Tulane Drama Review*, June, 1961. Largely philosophical and historical, this essay may help the actor think through the intellectual side of his work.

Selden, Samuel. *First Steps in Acting*. New York: Appleton-Century-Crofts, 1947. A technical approach with emphasis on image, pantomime, and speech. The book includes scenes for acting and an excellent collection of exercises.

Shank, Theodore J. *A Digest of 500 Plays*. New York: Crowell-Collier, 1963. This book is very handy if you wish to obtain information about a great many plays of high quality. It lists the number of male and female characters in each play.

Skinner, Cornelia Otis. *Family Circle*. Boston: Houghton-Mifflin, 1948. A delightful account of how this fine actress grew up in a loving family of theatrical geniuses.

Sorell, Walter (ed.). *The Dance Has Many Faces*. New York: Columbia University Press, 1968. Essays on the dance written by the best-known artists and including an extensive variety of subjects. An unusually fine collection.

Spolin, Viola. *Improvisation for the Theater*. Evanston: Northwestern University Press, 1963. This approach is rapidly becoming one of those most widely used for training actors. The book contains dozens of theatre games and exercises.

Stanislavsky, Constantin. *An Actor Prepares*. New York: Theatre Arts Books, 1936. The most famous book on "method" acting. It is written like a novel and presents complex ideas extremely clearly.

——————. *Building a Character*. New York: Theatre Arts Books, 1949. A valuable supplement to our book, containing many specific exercises for developing flexibility. This is the other side of method acting, the more technical side.

——————. *Creating a Role*. New York: Theatre Arts Books, 1961. An extraordinarily valuable book on how to approach creation of a specific role, based on detailed analyses of *Othello* and *The Inspector General*.

——————. *Stanislavsky on the Art of the Stage*. New York: Hill and Wang, 1961. A more theoretical book on acting than the other Stanislavsky books. David Magarshack's long introduction provides helpful interpretation. Also included are accounts of five rehearsals of *Werther*.

Strasberg, Lee. "Working with Live Material," *Tulane Drama Review*, Fall, 1964. The leading American exponent of method acting tries to clear up misconceptions about his work.

Strickland, F. Cowles. *The Technique of Acting*. New York: McGraw-Hill, 1956. One of the best texts on the subject. The emphasis is on technique and deals with such problems as timing and building a climax. Conscious design rather than psychological introspection is the keynote.

Terry, Ellen and Bernard Shaw. *A Correspondence*. New York: The Fountain Press, 1931. These letters, written without thought of publication, reveal something of the inner life as well as the art of a great actress and a great dramatist.

Terry, Walter. *Isadora Duncan: Her Life, Her Art, Her Legacy*. New York: Dodd, Mead, 1964. An excellent biography of the woman who first dared to "dance life's impulses." A personal view of the beginnings of modern dance.

Tompkins, Peter (ed.). *To a Young Actress: The Letters of Bernard Shaw to Molly Tompkins*. New York: Clarkson N. Potter, 1960. Shaw's early letters to this American actress who captured his fancy read like a course in acting.

Trewin, J. C. (ed.). *The Journal of William Charles Macready*. Carbondale: Southern Illinois University Press, 1967. One of the principal figures in the drama and literature of the early nineteenth century reveals his daily life as an actor.

Tynan, Kenneth. "The Actor: Tynan interviews Olivier," *Tulane Drama Review*, Winter, 1966. A lengthy and revealing glimpse of Britain's finest actor.

Wagner, Arthur. "Transactional Analysis and Acting," *Tulane Drama Review*, Summer, 1967. Develops an awareness of differences between social and psychological levels of action in characters.

Walker, Kathrine Sorley. *Eyes on Mime*. New York: The John Day Company, 1969. For the general reader rather than the student, this book refers to many exercises without specifying them.

Watkins, Ronald. *On Producing Shakespeare*. New York: W. W. Norton, 1950. This book has influenced the physical arrangement of many modern productions of Shakespeare. It is one of the best explanations of the effect of the theatre on the plays.

West, E. J. (ed.). *Shaw on Theatre*. New York: Hill and Wang, 1958. Some of Shaw's best and least-known critical writings. Particularly fascinating are the articles on the Shakespearean actor, Barry Sullivan.

Whiting, Frank M. *An Introduction to the Theatre*. New York: Harper, 1954. Has a chapter on the history of acting.

Williams, Raymond. *Drama in Performance*. London: C. A. Watts, 1968. *Antigone, Antony and Cleopatra, The Seagull*, and *Wild Strawberries* are discussed in terms of their original productions. A good book for helping to understand the interrelationship between actor, theatre, and play.

Wilson, Garff B. *A History of American Acting*. Bloomington, Indiana University Press, 1966. A scholarly book, emphasizing the nineteenth century.

Yurka, Blanche. *Dear Audience*. Englewood

Cliffs, Prentice-Hall, 1959. A chatty and delightful book by a great acting teacher.

BOOKS ON MAINTAINING GENERAL PHYSICAL CONDITION

Cooper, Kenneth H., M.D., M.P.H., Major, U.S.A.F. Medical Corps. *Aerobics*. New York: Bantam Books, 1968. It is essential to exercise a certain amount each week. This book allows you to choose from many kinds of exercise and tells you how much of each kind is needed.

Davis, Adelle. *Let's Eat Right to Keep Fit*. New York: Harcourt, Brace and World, 1954. Popular American eating habits are not conducive to good health. This book can help you revise your diet so that you will feel better most of the time. Its approach is complex, involving foods of all kinds; and it is not to be confused with the simplistic thinking of faddists.

Huffaker, Stephen. *The I Hate to Exercise Book*. New York: Pocket Books, 1970. If you haven't the will power to follow through on Aerobics, at least do the exercises prescribed here on the theory that something is better than nothing.

Kraskin, Robert A. *You Can Improve Your Vision*. New York: Doubleday, 1968. Provides a theoretical basis for protecting and improving your vision.

Leverton, Ruth M. *Food Becomes You*. New York: Dolphin Books, 1961. More conservative than Davis' book, this offers a sound scientific approach to nutrition.

Royal Canadian Air Force. *Exercise Plans for Physical Fitness*. New York: Pocket Books, 1962. A program of calesthenics progressive in difficulty, designed to help you build your physical fitness in an orderly manner. This book should be used in conjunction with *Aerobics*. It is to be preferred to any program designed to build muscles through weight lifting or isometrics, both of which may have deleterious effects on general physical fitness.

Selye, Hans. *The Stress of Life*. New York: McGraw-Hill Paperbacks, 1956. You may not wish to read all of this book, but if you follow the author's suggestions on what portions of it to read first, you will attain a theoretical understanding of how your body adapts to stress that will greatly facilitate planning an intelligent program of physical development.

Wikler, Simon J. *Take Off Your Shoes and Walk*. New York: Devin-Adair, 1961. Poorly fitting shoes can cripple your feet and impair your general health. This book will help you make sure that you are wearing the proper shoes and thus provide you with a very simple way of improving your physical condition.